MACMILLAN MAS

C000015544

GENERAL EDITOR: JAMES GIBSON

Published

JANE AUSTEN	*Emma* Norman Page
	Persuasion Judy Simons
	Sense and Sensibility Judy Simons
	Pride and Prejudice Raymond Wilson
	Mansfield Park Richard Wirdnam
SAMUEL BECKETT	*Waiting for Godot* Jennifer Birkett
WILLIAM BLAKE	*Songs of Innocence* and *Songs of Experience* Alan Tomlinson
ROBERT BOLT	*A Man for all Seasons* Leonard Smith
EMILY BRONTË	*Wuthering Heights* Hilda D. Spear
GEOFFREY CHAUCER	*The Miller's Tale* Michael Alexander
	The Pardoner's Tale Geoffrey Lester
	The Wife of Bath's Tale Nicholas Marsh
	The Knight's Tale Anne Samson
	The Prologue to the Canterbury Tales Nigel Thomas and Richard Swan
JOSEPH CONRAD	*The Secret Agent* Andrew Mayne
CHARLES DICKENS	*Bleak House* Dennis Butts
	Great Expectations Dennis Butts
	Hard Times Norman Page
GEORGE ELIOT	*Middlemarch* Graham Handley
	Silas Marner Graham Handley
	The Mill on the Floss Helen Wheeler
HENRY FIELDING	*Joseph Andrews* Trevor Johnson
E. M. FORSTER	*Howards End* Ian Milligan
	A Passage to India Hilda D. Spear
WILLIAM GOLDING	*The Spire* Rosemary Sumner
	Lord of the Flies Raymond Wilson
OLIVER GOLDSMITH	*She Stoops to Conquer* Paul Ranger
THOMAS HARDY	*The Mayor of Casterbridge* Ray Evans
	Tess of the d'Urbervilles James Gibson
	Far from the Madding Crowd Colin Temblett-Wood
GERARD MANLEY HOPKINS	*Selected Poems* R. J. C. Watt
JOHN KEATS	*Selected Poems* John Garrett
PHILIP LARKIN	*The Whitsun Weddings* and *The Less Deceived* Andrew Swarbrick
D. H. LAWRENCE	*Sons and Lovers* R. P. Draper
HARPER LEE	*To Kill a Mockingbird* Jean Armstrong
CHRISTOPHER MARLOWE	*Doctor Faustus* David A. Male
THE METAPHYSICAL POETS	Joan van Emden

MACMILLAN MASTER GUIDES

THOMAS MIDDLETON and WILLIAM ROWLEY	*The Changeling* Tony Bromham
ARTHUR MILLER	*The Crucible* Leonard Smith *Death of a Salesman* Peter Spalding
GEORGE ORWELL	*Animal Farm* Jean Armstrong
WILLIAM SHAKESPEARE	*Richard II* Charles Barber *Hamlet* Jean Brooks *King Lear* Francis Casey *Henry V* Peter Davison *The Winter's Tale* Diana Devlin *Julius Caesar* David Elloway *Macbeth* David Elloway *Measure for Measure* Mark Lilly *Henry IV Part I* Helen Morris *Romeo and Juliet* Helen Morris *A Midsummer Night's Dream* Kenneth Pickering *The Tempest* Kenneth Pickering *Coriolanus* Gordon Williams *Antony and Cleopatra* Martin Wine
GEORGE BERNARD SHAW	*St Joan* Leonée Ormond
RICHARD SHERIDAN	*The School for Scandal* Paul Ranger *The Rivals* Jeremy Rowe
ALFRED TENNYSON	*In Memoriam* Richard Gill
ANTHONY TROLLOPE	*Barchester Towers* K. M. Newton
JOHN WEBSTER	*The White Devil* and *The Duchess of Malfi* David A. Male
VIRGINIA WOOLF	*To the Lighthouse* John Mepham *Mrs Dalloway* Julian Pattison

Forthcoming

CHARLOTTE BRONTË	*Jane Eyre* Robert Miles
JOHN BUNYAN	*The Pilgrim's Progress* Beatrice Batson
T. S. ELIOT	*Murder in the Cathedral* Paul Lapworth *Selected Poems* Andrew Swarbrick
BEN JONSON	*Volpone* Michael Stout
RUDYARD KIPLING	*Kim* Leonée Ormond
JOHN MILTON	*Comus* Tom Healy
WILLIAM SHAKESPEARE	*Othello* Tony Bromham *As You Like It* Kiernan Ryan
W. B. YEATS	*Selected Poems* Stan Smith

MACMILLAN MASTER GUIDES

PERSUASION

BY JANE AUSTEN

JUDY SIMONS

MACMILLAN
EDUCATION

First edition 1987

Published by
MACMILLAN EDUCATION LTD
Houndmills, Basingstoke, Hampshire RG21 2XS
and London
Companies and representatives
throughout the world

Phototypeset by
TecSet Limited, Wallington, Surrey

Printed in Hong Kong

British Library Cataloguing in Publication Data
Simons, Judy
Persuasion by Jane Austen.—(Macmillan
master guides).
1. Austen, Jane. Persuasion
I. Title   II. Austen, Jane
823'.7   PR4034.P43
ISBN 0–333–44606–2 Pbk
ISBN 0–333–44607–0 Pbk export

CONTENTS

GENERAL EDITOR'S PREFACE

The aim of the Macmillan Master Guides is to help you to appreciate the book you are studying by providing information about it and by suggesting ways of reading and thinking about it which will lead to a fuller understanding. The section on the writer's life and background has been designed to illustrate those aspects of the writer's life which have influenced the work, and to place it in its personal and literary context. The summaries and critical commentary are of special importance in that each brief summary of the action is followed by an examination of the significant critical points. The space which might have been given to repetitive explanatory notes has been devoted to a detailed analysis of the kind of passage which might confront you in an examination. Literary criticism is concerned with both the broader aspects of the work being studied and with its detail. The ideas which meet us in reading a great work of literature, and their relevance to us today, are an essential part of our study, and our Guides look at the thought of their subject in some detail. But just as essential is the craft with which the writer has constructed his work of art, and this may be considered under several technical headings − characterisation, language, style and stagecraft, for example.

The authors of these Guides are all teachers and writers of wide experience, and they have chosen to write about books they admire and know well in the belief that they can communicate their admiration to you. But you yourself must read and know intimately the book you are studying. No one can do that for you. You should see this book as a lamp-post. Use it to shed light, not to lean against. If you know your text and know what it is saying about life, and how it says it, then you will enjoy it, and there is no better way of passing an examination in literature.

JAMES GIBSON

Acknowledgement

Cover illustration: *Dining Room at Langton Hall: Family at Breakfast* by Mary Ellen Best. Photograph © Caroline Davidson and by courtesy of Bridgeman Art Library.

1 JANE AUSTEN: LIFE AND BACKGROUND

Jane Austen was born in Steventon, Hampshire on 16 December 1775. She was the seventh of eight children of George and Cassandra Austen and she grew up with her brothers and sisters in a warm and secure family atmosphere. She was particularly close to her older sister, Cassandra, whose bedroom she shared and from whom she could not bear to be parted. She also had a favourite brother, Henry, supposedly the most charming of the Austens, who was four years older than Jane and on whom she relied for advice. The surviving correspondence of Jane Austen, which is one of our main sources of information about her life, shows the importance to her of maintaining family contact. Almost all the letters, written from 1796 onwards, are to her sister, brothers and their children and contain the sort of gossip to be found in most families. Similarly, Jane Austen's novels always deal centrally with family relationships. The bonds between parents and children and brothers and sisters meant a lot to her, and she is harsh in her condemnation of characters (like the Elliots in *Persuasion*) who are cold-hearted and seem deficient in natural family feeling.

Although Jane Austen's family were not wealthy, they were comfortably off – Jane's father, the Reverend George Austen, was Rector of the small village of Steventon – and the children did not want for material comforts. They were part of the class known then as the 'gentry', what today we would probably call the English upper middle class, and it is this class which figures almost exclusively in all her novels, the class to which, in *Persuasion*, the Musgroves, the Crofts and Wentworth belong. Sir Walter Elliot, as a member of the minor aristocracy, is at one extreme of this 'gentry' grouping, while a character like Mrs Smith, who is of good birth but impoverished, is at the other. The Reverend Austen's relatives were successful business-men, landowners and professional men. Jane's mother, Cassandra Austen (née Leigh), was from a similar if rather more distinguished background, and together the parents provided for Jane and the other children a settled and well ordered environment for growing up, dominated by a belief in the value of good sense and a practical, humane education.

In 1782, Jane and Cassandra went to a small girls' boarding school in Oxford which later moved to Southampton, but when illness struck the school they were removed at once, and after a brief period at another school in Reading, they came home permanently. From the age of about eleven Jane Austen never left her family circle for any length of time. No wonder that her heroine, Anne Elliot, is so distressed at being uprooted from the house she has lived in all her life. We must not think that Jane Austen was badly educated, however, merely because she was taught at home. It was in fact from her home life that she acquired the real education that was to inform her perceptions on life and combine with her natural genius to produce her distinctive character as a novelist. Home education probably offered her far more opportunities for serious learning and gave her a wider range of knowledge than any ladies' seminary could have done. George Austen was an excellent scholar and teacher. He had been a teacher at a boys' school and he took in resident tutorial pupils from high-class families in order to give them a solid grounding in the classics. Jane was thus in daily contact with the procedures of classical scholarship. She herself read widely in her father's extensive library – not just from the classical authors of Greece and Rome, but from more modern English writers as well.

Jane was familiar with the works of the eighteenth-century essay-ists, Joseph Addison, Richard Steele and her own particular favour-ite, Dr Samuel Johnson. All these writers specialised in pithy commentary on the world around them. They dealt not with heroes and heroines in the classical mould, but cast a stern eye on contem-porary morals, and it is this moral stance that provides the basis for Jane Austen's own books. She also loved reading novels, a literary form which was fairly recent in English and which was to have such a decisive influence on her. In the middle of the eighteenth century the two most famous novelists were Samuel Richardson (1689–1761) and

Henry Fielding (1707–54). Both were strong moralists, although with very different emphases. Richardson was a more serious, romantic writer who concentrated on love relationships and described the details of individual domestic lives. Fielding was a comic writer who used satire to expose the follies and vices of contemporary society. Jane Austen's own writing drew on both these sources, and we can see the evidence of this in *Persuasion*, which mixes these two traditions, offering the reader an insight into the minute gradations of Anne Elliot's feelings set often in the most mundane surroundings, while also savagely satirising the vanity and snobbery of Sir Walter Elliot and his cronies.

But the books which had the most formative influence on Jane Austen's literary development were the novels produced by women writers. Women were in many ways a disadvantaged sex in the late eighteenth and early nineteenth centuries without the equality that we take for granted today. Girls did not normally have the same sort of education as boys: their schools concentrated on 'accomplishments' such as drawing, music, sewing and perhaps a little French, rather than the masculine rigours of mathematics, history or Latin. Nor did women have the same financial independence or rights of inheritance as men. It was one of George Austen's sons, Jane's brother Edward, not one of his daughters, who was chosen as heir to a wealthy relative, Thomas Knight. The Austen girls did not have the opportunity to go to university like their brothers or to make a career for themselves when they grew up. While her brothers went into the Navy (two of them became Admirals), the Army and the Church, Jane and Cassandra were expected to stay at home quietly, busying themselves with housekeeping until some young man might make them an offer of marriage. When George Austen died in 1805, Jane, her mother and sister were left with a very meagre income of £210 per year, and would have found it extremely difficult to manage had it not been for the kindness of her brothers who were able to help them out. Although Jane did earn a little money from her novels, this was only in the last six years of her life and she never thought of writing as her full-time job. She wrote only when her domestic duties were finished with, and she always put her work away when visitors arrived, slipping it under a convenient blotting pad on the desk in the family sitting room. The portrayal of Anne Elliot emphasises some of these disadvantages. Anne is, for instance, totally dependent on others and has no money of her own. Even her family home is left to a distant male relative who has never set eyes on the place rather than to Sir Walter's daughters, none of whom can inherit either his title or his property. We should also bear in mind that Anne cannot speak directly to Wentworth or propose marriage. She has to wait to be asked: anything else would have been unthinkable at that period.

When novels by women writers began to appear towards the end of the eighteenth century, Jane Austen devoured them eagerly, finding in their pages a representation of women's experience, written from a woman's point of view. Often these novels were very silly – she parodies some of their more ridiculous features in her high-spirited early work, *Love and Freindship*, written when she was still a teenager. But many more fired her imagination; by showing her what women were capable of achieving, they had a profound influence on her own writing. Jane Austen admired the work of Fanny Burney, whose *Evelina* (1778) was a sparkling comic novel in letters describing a young country girl's first encounter with London life. She also read the books of Charlotte Smith, exciting romances featuring heroines who combined an active intelligence with the requisite perfection of the feeling heart. But these women were exceptional, and it was still a relatively new occurrence to find women publishing novels at all in this period. When Anne Elliot speaks to Captain Harville in Chapter 23 of *Persuasion* about the drawbacks of being a woman, she comments feelingly on the fact that women have not had the same opportunities as men of expressing themselves in print.

The Austen family was a lively one. Its members were clever, active and articulate, and all seem to have possessed a strong sense of humour. The boys threw themselves into outdoor pursuits such as riding, shooting and hunting, but with their sisters and assorted cousins they also enjoyed amateur theatricals, and from an early age Jane took part in acting and writing for these private performances, which were almost invariably comedies. Her keen ear for speech patterns and her fine dramatic inventiveness stayed with her throughout her life, and many of her novels contain sections that read almost like plays in the wit and sparkle of their comic dialogue and the farcical scenes they create.

Although Jane stayed at home for most of her adult life, she took a keen interest in the careers of her brothers, and it is characteristically these careers (as sailors, soldiers or clergymen) that the men in her novels adopt: characteristically, because Jane Austen only wrote about matters she knew well. She followed the progress of her two sailor brothers, Charles and Frank, from their humble beginnings as midshipmen through their various stages to the elevated rank of Admiral. Several of her letters deal with the procedures and difficulties of naval promotion. 'Frank is made', she wrote delightedly to Cassandra in December 1798. 'He was yesterday raised to the Rank of Commander & appointed to the Petterel Sloop, now at Gibralter.' She was able to portray with confidence the sailor's life which figures so prominently in *Persuasion*, and the anxieties which sailors' wives and sweethearts experience were those which she and her family had undergone in worrying about Frank's safety during the battles of the Napoleonic wars. Clearly her personal involvement in seafaring life, its adventures and excitements affected her choice of Wentworth as the charismatic hero who has experienced dangers but has won glory and fortune through his personal courage and skill.

In 1801 Jane Austen's father retired from his position as rector and decided to take his wife and daughters to live in Bath. His sudden decision came out of the blue to the girls, and Jane fainted on hearing the news. All her life Jane Austen valued stability and disliked change. Also at this time she was suffering from an illness which we now know as Addison's Disease, which ultimately was to prove fatal, and which would have contributed to her violent reaction to her father's announcement. In Bath, the Austens stayed in lodgings similar to those described in *Persuasion*. Jane Austen's letters from Bath give the impression of a place populated by self-important, dull characters. 'Another stupid party last night' is a typical comment in a letter of 1801. 'Perhaps if larger, they might be less intolerable, but here there were only just enough to make one card table with six people to look on and talk nonsense to each other.' It is just this sort of vapid existence that Anne Elliot finds Sir Walter full of when she arrives in Bath, and in *Persuasion* we find a harsh portrait of a city which was once thought to be the height of elegance and sophistication.

It was during the period spent in Bath that Jane Austen visited Lyme Regis, the town which plays such a crucial part in *Persuasion*. It was about this time too, on another visit to the seaside, that she met a young clergyman and they fell in love. According to the story told long afterwards by Cassandra, he was 'one of the most charming persons she had ever known', but his sudden death shortly after this first meeting put a tragic end to the love affair. Jane Austen would have been about twenty-seven, the age of her heroine Anne Elliot, when all this happened. It is significant that no letters of hers survive from this period. After her sister's death, Cassandra went through her correspondence and destroyed anything she thought too intimate for others' eyes. As a result we can only guess at the suffering and the sadness that lay beneath the surface of the casual gossip and family news with which the existing letters are filled. *Persuasion* itself perhaps offers the most revealing insights into Jane Austen's understanding of love, and the hints of tragic accidents that pervade the novel might well point to the experiences in her own life that have remained secret.

In 1806, after George Austen's death, his widow and daughters stayed in temporary accommodation until they eventually settled in Chawton, in a cottage adjoining Edward's estate, and it was here Jane Austen lived until her death. The bulk of her three early books, *Sense and Sensibility* (1795), *Pride and Prejudice* (1796) and *Northanger Abbey* (1798) was written while she lived at Steventon, but all three were amended during her Chawton years, and *Sense and Sensibility* and *Pride and Prejudice* were published from there in 1811 and 1812 respectively. *Mansfield Park* (1814) and *Emma* (1815) were her next two novels. By this stage, she had built up something of a literary reputation, and on hearing that the Prince Regent (later to become King George IV) admired her work, she was encouraged to dedicate *Emma* to him. She began work on *Persuasion* on 8 August 1815 and completed the first version of the book just under a year later on 18 July 1816. She then spent some time in substantially revising her first draft, although the illness from which she had been suffering for some years was by now greatly debilitating. Despite growing progressively weaker, she also began another novel, *Sanditon*, but this was never to be completed. In the spring of 1817, she moved with Cassandra to Winchester in order to be near a good doctor, but in July she died in her sister's arms. *Persuasion* was published, together with *Northanger Abbey*, the following December. When we read Jane Austen's novels now, we can identify a distinct difference in tone between the three Steventon novels and those produced at Chawton. *Sense and Sensibility*, *Pride and Prejudice* and *Northanger Abbey* are, as Jane Austen herself described one of them, 'light and bright and sparkling', overflowing with a spirit of mischievous fun. The more mature novels of the Chawton years contain hints of an underlying sadness while still conforming to the comic mode, and *Persuasion*, her last completed work, is built around a close interweaving of comic and serious elements. The two periods that dominate Jane Austen's artistic career coincide with the period of cultural change that was taking place around her. The 1790s saw the growth of the Romantic movement throughout Europe. In England two of its leading exponents were William Wordsworth and Samuel Taylor Coleridge, whose poetry of these years celebrated the beauties of Nature and asserted the value of individual feeling in determining the truth of experience. Their first collection of poetry, *Lyrical Ballads* (1798), dwelt on the level of insight attainable through intuition and spontaneous feeling and suggested that rationalist systematic thought was unreliable and constricting. The earlier eighteenth-century belief in the power of Reason was seen as misguided, and a new philosophy based on the power of Imagination took its place. Much of Jane Austen's early work seems to be in conflict with this attitude. In satirising Romantic extremism, she appears to be arguing for moderation, good sense and a belief in established order. *Persuasion*, however, is a novel written when Romanticism could no longer be dismissed as a literary fad, and the text shows a great deal of sympathy with Romantic ideals. The descriptions of natural surroundings and the use of autumnal imagery have a direct correlation with the techniques of contemporary poetry, and the central narrative strand focuses more intensively on a personal love story than any of Jane Austen's earlier novels.

Romanticism was in many ways the literary corollary to the changes that were taking place in the social and political climate of Jane Austen's world. At the turn of the nineteenth century, English society was gradually moving away from the feudal agricultural base that had supported it for generations to a more modern industrial society with a greater scope for social mobility. The American Revolution in 1776, when the states of North America established their independence from the British government, and the French Revolution of 1789, when the ordinary people of France broke away from what they felt was the tyranny of monarchy and established a republic, had a deep influence on the political awareness of the English gentry. Both revolutions were based on associated ideals of individual liberty, equality and the brotherhood of man, and their success demonstrated that royal sovereignty was not a political necessity and that the hierarchy of social class was not infallible. Although the changes in English society were far more insidious and less violent than those abroad, radical views inevitably inform Jane

Austen's perception, and as a social historian she records the processes of the shifting society in which she lived. So, in *Persuasion*, the representative of the old aristocratic order, Sir Walter Elliot, is compelled to give up his ancestral home to the new forces of energetic, professional individualism, represented by Admiral Croft.

It is often alleged that Jane Austen portrays a narrow world in her fiction because she restricts herself to the activities of one social class. But it is a mistake to equate her choice of artistic material with a corresponding narrowness of vision. She chose her field quite deliberately and was fully aware of what she was doing. In one letter to her brother, Edward, she compared her writing to a 'little bit (two inches wide) of Ivory, on which I work with so fine a Brush, as produces little effect after much labour.' We need to recognise that the band of society she selects for her fiction is used to chart the much larger movements of historical change. Constantly Jane Austen shows us individuals who are victims of social circumstances, people who have come down in the world and others who are rapidly rising in importance. Her descriptions of setting also emphasise the way in which the English landscape is constantly changing, and this reflects the processes of human history which form a context for the individual stories of her novels.

2 SUMMARIES

AND

CRITICAL COMMENTARY

2.1 OVERALL PLOT SYNOPSIS

The snobbish Sir Walter Elliot, a widower of Kellynch Hall, has three daughters, Elizabeth and Anne, who are both unmarried, and Mary, who is married to a neighbour, Charles Musgrove. Eight years earlier, Anne was betrothed to a young naval officer, Captain Frederick Wentworth, but she was persuaded by her family and a close friend of her late mother, Lady Russell, to break the engagement because of Wentworth's lack of prospects. She has regretted this decision ever since as she has never loved anyone but Wentworth. Increasing debts force Sir Walter to rent Kellynch Hall to Admiral Croft and his wife, who is Captain Wentworth's sister. Sir Walter goes to live in Bath with Elizabeth and a friend of hers, the widowed Mrs Clay, who is the daughter of Sir Walter's lawyer, Mr Shepherd. Anne stays behind, first with Lady Russell, and then with her sister Mary in the nearby village of Uppercross.

While staying with Mary and Charles, Anne is frequently in the company of Charles's family, Mr and Mrs Musgrove and their daughters, Henrietta and Louisa. Their only son, Richard, died at sea, serving on board a ship captained by Wentworth. When the Crofts settle in Kellynch, Captain Wentworth, who is now wealthy having been more successful in the Navy than had been thought likely, comes for an extended visit and the two families are in close daily contact. Wentworth seems attracted to both Henrietta and Louisa and treats Anne with cold formality. When Henrietta is courted by her cousin, Charles Hayter, Wentworth's attentions are devoted to Louisa, much to Anne's distress.

Joining a large party on a visit to Lyme Regis to see a friend of Wentworth's, Captain Harville, Anne attracts the attentions both of a passing stranger and of Harville's friend, Captain Benwick, who is in mourning for his late fiancée, Harville's sister, Fanny. While out walking in Lyme, Louisa Musgrove has a bad fall and suffers severe concussion. In the ensuing panic, Anne takes control of the situation. When the others return to Uppercross, Louisa remains in Lyme to recuperate.

Shortly afterwards, Anne, accompanied by Lady Russell, goes to Bath to stay with her father. Sir Walter and Elizabeth have become friendly with their previously estranged cousin, Mr William Elliott, who is heir to the Kellynch estate. When they are introduced, Mr Elliot recognises Anne as the stranger he admired in Lyme. Sir Walter and Elizabeth also court the acquaintance of another distant, dull but prestigious relative, Lady Dalrymple, while Anne renews a friendship with Mrs Smith, an old schoolfriend whom she has discovered living in Bath, widowed, ill and in reduced circumstances. Anne is worried by the continued presence of Mrs Clay, whom she suspects of having designs on Sir Walter. Mr Elliot seems deeply attracted to Anne, and Lady Russell, among others, expects him to propose marriage. Anne receives a letter from Mary telling her that Louisa Musgrove has become engaged to Captain Benwick, and shortly afterwards Captain Wentworth arrives in Bath. The relationship between Wentworth and Anne daily grows more intimate, although there are still innumerable obstacles in the way of a full understanding, not least Mr Elliot's assiduous attentions to Anne.

Mary, Charles, Mrs Musgrove, Henrietta and Captain Harville arrive in Bath unexpectedly, to Anne's delight. One morning in their company, after talking to Captain Harville about woman's constancy, Anne is overwhelmed to receive a hastily written letter from Wentworth asking her to be his wife. Anne and Wentworth marry and become fully reconciled to Lady Russell. Mrs Clay goes to live with Mr Elliot, and Mrs Smith, her fortunes restored through Wentworth's efforts, stays a close friend.

2.2 CHAPTER SUMMARIES AND COMMENTARIES

Introductory note

When *Persuasion* was first printed in 1818, it was divided into two volumes of twelve chapters each. Most modern editions number the chapters consecutively 1–24, and this is the procedure I have followed for this Guide. All modern editions follow the same text, based on the standard edition of Jane Austen's works by R. W. Chapman of 1926. You might like to use the Macmillan Students Novel edition of *Persuasion*: the page references in Section 5 are to this text.

Chapter 1

The book opens with a description of the snobbish Sir Walter Elliot of Kellynch Hall, a widower with three daughters, Elizabeth, Anne and Mary. During the thirteen years since his wife's death, a close family friend, Lady Russell, has helped him bring up his children. His favourite is the eldest, Elizabeth, still unmarried despite his hopes that their cousin Mr William Walter Elliot, also a widower, would court her. He has no time for his second daughter, Anne, who is 27 and also unmarried, but is content that Mary has found a wealthy husband in their neighbour, Charles Musgrove. Heavy debts have forced Sir Walter to mortgage part of his estate, and his expenses continue to be heavy.

Commentary
The portrait of Sir Walter with which the novel begins presents him as obsessed with past glories and personal vanity. It is savagely iro-nic – the opening passage in particular forms a brilliant exposé of a man whose snobbery blinds him to the changing world in which he lives – and sets the tone for the false, uncaring environment in which the heroine, Anne Elliot, is to be found. Jane Austen's description of a father and his three daughters suggests an ironic re-telling of a traditional fairytale, a Cinderella-type story in which the heroine's true worth is disregarded by her family. Lady Russell is the only one to appreciate Anne as she deserves. Elizabeth's pride effectively aligns her with her father against Anne, whose personal qualities form a sharp contrast with the brittle status-conscious world that surrounds her. That this world is on its way out is indicated by the

decline in Sir Walter's fortunes and his refusal to understand his changing circumstances. Yet, despite the seriousness of the subject matter, we should note the variety of comic tones that Jane Austen brings to this chapter. Note especially the skilful use of detail, for instance in Elizabeth's proposals for economy, and the way in which Jane Austen recreates the speech patterns of reprehensible characters in order to render them ridiculous. The chapter is structured around what is to become a recurrent feature of the novel, the interaction of past, present and future time, so that all events are framed by what went before and by what might occur subsequently. The introduction of Mr William Walter Elliot at this early stage prepares us for his subsequent appearance.

Chapter 2

In the interests of economy, Sir Walter is persuaded by his lawyer, Mr Shepherd, and by Lady Russell, to let Kellynch Hall and to move to Bath. Lady Russell hopes that this move will also put an end to a friendship that has been growing between Elizabeth Elliot and Mr Shepherd's daughter, the sycophantic Mrs Clay.

Commentary
This chapter highlights the selfishness, blindness and pride of Sir Walter. He is impervious to reasoned argument and can only be persuaded to act after some careful handling by Lady Russell and Mr Shepherd – it should be noticed how this fits in to the pattern of 'persuasion' that is being built up throughout the novel. We also see here how Anne's wishes are constantly ignored in the decisions made about the family's future. The moral framework of the book is established, giving us clear guidelines as to the 'good' and 'bad' characters in the story. Can you see how this is done? Once again the effect comes partly from the dramatisation of individual personalities. For example, Mr Shepherd is distinguished by his over-careful use of language, as this is comically juxtaposed with the representation of Sir Walter's and Elizabeth's outrage after Lady Russell's tentative suggestions about economising. The chapter provides a continual interplay of perspectives, so that the foolish characters are set in a context created by the author's more reasoned comments. Note, however, the ambivalence regarding Lady Russell's position. She is not so easy to place in a moral category – she is

'good' because she is sympathetic to Anne and sees the Elliots' deficiencies clearly, but she also displays her own insensitivity when she insists on taking Anne to Bath. This difficulty of categorisation has important thematic implications when we later try to judge her behaviour.

Chapter 3

Mr Shepherd finds a tenant for Kellynch Hall in Admiral Croft, a man who meets with Sir Walter's approval and who has connections with the neighbourhood, his wife's brother having been curate in a nearby village some years before.

Commentary
This is a most subtly worked chapter in which we can see the basis of Jane Austen's method in this novel. The focus is obstensibly on Sir Walter's foolish egoism, and the fun is gained from the satirical exposure of his stupidity and from watching the machinations of Mrs Clay and Mr Shepherd. Look at the effects of Jane Austen's interpolated comments, apparently casual but which give us the corrective on her characters. A phrase such as 'Mr Shepherd laughed, as he knew he must, at this wit' illuminates both Sir Walter's inanity and the lawyer's insincerity. However, beneath the sharp comic surface is another level of communication. Note Anne's heightened state of awareness *vis-à-vis* the discussions taking place around her: she defends the Navy; she seems to know all about Admiral Croft; and the final paragraph of the chapter directs us towards her consciousness, and towards her 'flushed cheeks', the outward sign of her inner turmoil. The division between moral types that we saw in Chapter 2 has developed to incorporate a division between different levels of experience: spoken and unspoken; public and private; shallow and deep. Note, too, the way in which this novel is given a precise historical dimension. Mr Shepherd's opening speech refers to the events of 1815, after England's triumph at the battle of Waterloo. Thus the effects of war in a distant land are felt by those at home. The relativism of time and place that the book demonstrates is reinforced by the smallest detail.

Chapter 4

The story goes back to describe an episode which took place nearly eight years before, when Anne became engaged to Captain Frederick Wentworth, who had been staying near Kellynch with his curate brother. Faced with the disapproval of her family, Anne was persuaded by Lady Russell to break the engagement and has not seen Wentworth since. Despite an offer of marriage from Charles Musgrove, she has never loved anyone but Wentworth, and is now nervous about the possibility of his return to Kellynch with the Crofts.

Commentary

This is where the story really begins! The hints regarding Anne in the previous chapter are now clarified. It is most unusual for Jane Austen to move her readers back in time in this way, but in this novel it is fundamental to the exploration of the relationship between past and present time which is one of its major concerns. You should examine the analysis of Anne's decision to reject Wentworth very carefully. What is it that ultimately persuades her to break the engagement? This is not a simple matter at all, and her decision is not one that is lightly taken. Note how the language first dramatises Lady Russell's opinions, rather overstated and melodramatic, almost as if she is trying to convince herself of the validity of her position. It is a hallmark of Jane Austen's technique that characters give themselves away through their use of language. The style then changes so that it is as if we are placed inside Anne's thought processes and can follow her own internal arguments. These are much more considered and self-denying, and form a contrast with Lady Russell's methods of reaching a conclusion. The attention of the novel is now clearly focused on Anne's state of mind and the growth in her understanding that these past eight years have effected. Unusually for a Jane Austen heroine, Anne Elliot is presented as mature from the beginning of the novel in her awareness of the complex nature of human experience and the variables that control it. You should note too how many words relating to feeling are associated with Anne here: her emotions, hidden from those around her, are continually active, and this is important in a text that is crucially concerned with what constitutes true feeling.

Chapter 5

Anne keeps out of the way when the Crofts call to inspect Kellynch. Sir Walter and Elizabeth move to Bath, having invited Mrs Clay to accompany them while leaving Anne behind to follow later. Anne tries to warn Elizabeth of her suspicions that Mrs Clay has designs on their father, but to no effect. After their departure, Anne spends a few days with Lady Russell and then goes to the neighbouring village of Uppercross to stay with her younger sister, Mary, who is unwell. They pay a visit to Mary's in-laws, Mr and Mrs Musgrove and their two daughters, Henrietta and Louisa.

Commentary
Again Anne's neglect by her father and elder sister is marked; their preference for the grasping Mrs Clay is blinkered and, like their attitude to their financial circumstances, is yet another example of their inability to foresee potential danger. The comments about Mrs Clay's plainness are more than a gesture towards caricature. Can you see how the idea of personal appearance takes on the status of a thematic motif, as references to physical attraction gradually accumulate? Even in these first five chapters we have been notified of Sir Walter's handsome features, Elizabeth's stultified beauty, Anne's faded looks and the effects of a seafaring life on the complexion. What do you think these signify?

Note the mingling of comic and serious elements in this chapter. The satire, so economically handled, is directed at Sir Walter, Elizabeth and the hypochondriacal Mary, who swiftly recovers from her illness when given some sympathetic attention. This chapter also contains the first real introduction to Mary as a character, and you should notice how her personality, distinguished by egoism, petulance and self-indulgence, is fully conveyed in the few lines of dialogue she is given. Her chatter is balanced by the treatment of Anne's quietness, which is shown to conceal great sensitivity, acute perception and a resigned acceptance of her helpless position.

In addition, the chapter provides a sense of the importance of place, in the description of the disruption caused to Anne by the removal from Kellynch. She is now bereft of love, family and a home, the embodiment of rootlessness. Her isolation, which has been a feature of her presentation from Chapter 1 onwards, is now becoming more and more marked.

Chapter 6

At Uppercross Anne finds that the Musgroves are totally absorbed in their affairs and are indifferent to her situation. The Crofts call on Mary, and Anne immediately warms to them. She is, however, disconcerted to learn that they expect a visit from Captain Wentworth shortly. The Musgroves realise that Wentworth was the captain under whom their late son, Richard, had served.

Commentary
The theme of human egoism, introduced in the first chapter with the extreme example of Sir Walter, is developed as we see how all individuals are to some degree self-absorbed. Anne is forced to realise the marginality of Kellynch affairs to those at Uppercross, and she has to adapt to the different situations in which she finds herself. The description of the Musgrove family relationships is at one level delightfully comic, as Mary and Mrs Musgrove each complain to Anne about each other's conduct. However, this has serious implications in showing how events are open to alternative interpretations. The idea of the relativism of perception is also suggested, and this is to become a major issue in the novel, as we are continually invited to see events from differing viewpoints. The text frequently stresses the supremacy of the subjective view for each individual. In the context of the active and lively Musgrove family, Anne's isolation becomes more emphatic – she is taken for granted by all around her, a willing ear for their troubles, a source of sympathy and advice, but they are insenitive to the existence of her own inner life. The introduction of the Crofts forces attention on the past, and this again becomes a significant issue. Mrs Musgrove re-interprets past events (the death of her son, Richard) according to her own memory, which is shown as fallible. Jane Austen's novels frequently satirise excess, and Mrs Musgrove's tendency towards false sentimentality is accordingly treated comically here. The more serious question of the relationship between memory and reality is raised through the contrast between Anne and Mrs Musgrove, and anticipates the return of Wentworth in the next chapter.

Chapter 7

Captain Wentworth, now wealthy and successful, arrives at Kellynch and is soon on intimate terms with the Musgroves. Mary's young son, Charles, has an accident and breaks his collar bone. Anne stays at home to look after him while the others go to dinner with Wentworth. Her first meeting with him, however, cannot be postponed indefinitely, and although brief it fills Anne with anxiety. Wentworth tells Mrs Croft that he now feels ready to get married and that he is seeking a wife who has a strong mind.

Commentary
One of the major ironies of *Persuasion* is that the central character is the most static, although she is placed firmly at the centre of the emotional action of the book. Here we learn about events as they are filtered through Anne's consciousness. It is her response that is in the foreground, and her violent emotions regarding the slightest details show us that her feelings for Wentworth dominate all aspects of her experience. Her agitation at the thought of meeting him again is extreme, and the meeting itself, although confined to curt formalities, leaves her deeply affected and dominates her thoughts. Yet this is all beneath the surface. None of the other characters can guess at Anne's inward feelings, which contrast with the decorousness and reticence of her outward behaviour. Jane Austen frequently invests apparent trivialities with great significance: here they are personalised so that Anne reads volumes into Wentworth's most casual action. You should note her profound response, for instance, on hearing his lightly expressed opinion about her altered looks. It is, incidentally, significant that this is reported to her by Mary, indifferent to the hurt she is inflicting. The final paragraphs of the chapter direct us to Wentworth's feelings. The pain he has suffered from the broken engagement is strongly implied, and the final words 'I have thought on the subject more than most men' are resonant with unuttered meaning that the reader, but not Mrs Croft, can infer.

Chapter 8

Captain Wentworth soon becomes the favourite of the Musgrove family, but his relations with Anne are strained and formal. One evening the general conversation about seafaring life includes rem-

iniscences of the Musgroves' late son Dick, and remarks about the
wisdom of ladies travelling on board ship.

Commentary
Persuasion is the most static of all Jane Austen's novels, and this
episode demonstrates the use made from the apparent lack of action.
It starts and ends with a comment on Anne's feelings, and these
frame the social chit-chat which intervenes and reminds us that
although she takes no active part in it, Anne is an alert and fully
involved participant. Despite her depth of understanding, however,
Anne is still not able to foresee the future pattern of events: she is
convinced at this stage that she and Wentworth 'could never become
acquainted. It was a perpetual estrangement.' Throughout the novel
the point is made that human vision is inevitably limited, and that
nothing can be predicted with certainty. Yet although Anne is to be
proved wrong by subsequent developments, this in no way undermines the status of her judgement in comparison with the other
characters.

The chapter gives us the first direct view of Captain Wentworth (I
deal with this more fully in Section 5). His behaviour towards Anne is
an indication of the strength of his bitterness: the excessive formality
with which he treats her at the end of the scene suggests the power of
memory for him, as well as for her, as it forms such a deliberate
contrast with the remembered intimacy of their former relationship.
Past and present action is thus juxtaposed. The conversations about
death and nostalgia (*vis-à-vis* Dick Musgrove) and about marriage
(*vis-à-vis* the Crofts) relate to two of the main thematic strands of the
novel, and we can see how these ideas recur throughout the book.
The interchange between Mrs Musgrove and Mrs Croft anticipates
their conversation in Chapter 23. Jane Austen structures the novel
around parallel incidents which form a subtle pattern of cross-
reference. On each occasion the two ladies, who are minor (and in
Mrs Musgrove's case ridiculous) characters, are overheard, first by
Anne and then by Wentworth, with dramatic consequences.

Chapter 9

Much to Anne's discomfiture, Charles and Mary Musgrove discuss
the possibility of Wentworth's marrying Louisa or Henrietta. The
situation is complicated by the appearance of Charles Hayter, a

cousin of the Musgroves who has been courting Henrietta. One morning Wentworth arrives at Uppercross and finds himself unexpectedly alone with Anne and the sick child she is looking after. A few minutes later Charles Hayter and Mary's other son arrive. When the children become troublesome, Wentworth goes silently to Anne's aid.

Commentary

Marriage, in both its public and private dimensions, forms the main subject of this episode. The author's opening description of the Musgrove and Hayter families is amplified by the discussion between Charles and Mary, where Mary's social pretensions and narrow criteria of judgement are caricatured. Her views on marriage form a neat contrast with those of Mrs Musgrove and Mrs Croft in the last chapter. It is especially ironic that Mary should be promoting Wentworth's case on social grounds, given the Elliots' dismissal of him eight years previously.

Once again we see how minutiae are used to carry weight, as in the incident with little Charles. Anne's violent reaction to Wentworth's action indicates the power of the bond she still feels exists between them and emphasises retrospectively the pain she must undergo when compelled to discuss which sister he is in love with. Wentworth's positive role contrasts with Charles Hayter's negative one and, as well as demonstrating the difference between the two men, indicates his unspoken awareness of Anne's situation, his sensitivity to her distress, and the active nature of his compassion. Note Anne's silence throughout this chapter. Noise and confusion take place all around her, but her activity is all internal.

Chapter 10

Anne, Mary, Henrietta, Louisa, Charles Musgrove and Captain Wentworth go for a walk, during which Anne overhears a conversation between Wentworth and Louisa. Louisa declares her belief in lovers' constancy, and Wentworth, clearly admiring her attitude, extols the virtues of decision and firmness of mind which she seems to embody. Charles Hayter joins the party and his intimacy with Henrietta marks out Louisa for Wentworth's sole attentions. The Crofts pass in their carriage and offer a lift to anyone who might be tired. Before she has a chance to speak, Anne is helped into the carriage by Wentworth.

Commentary

This episode is shot through with multiple ironies, many of which relate fundamentally to the concept of 'persuasion'. The central conversation between Louisa and Wentworth about decisiveness is undercut by the decisions which surround it. Look at all the ways in which the characters make choices. From the initial decisions about who will go on the walk (Mary, for instance, only joins them because they try to dissuade her) to Wentworth's 'choice' of Louisa, determined by circumstances outside his control (note the Crofts' comment that he can't make up his own mind), and Anne's final acceptance of the Crofts' offer, which she was in the process of refusing, actions are seen to be subject to a variety of causes; we are shown that 'persuasion' comes in many guises. Wentworth's speech to Louisa about the hazelnut is doubly ironic: the qualities he describes are more appropriate to Anne than to Louisa, whose declaration about constancy is overturned by later events. Not only does this invite a comparison between Anne and Louisa, but it suggests Wentworth's own lack of discernment at this stage in the novel. Louisa's interpretation of Anne's refusal of Charles Musgrove's proposal of marriage adds to the complicated pattern of misunderstanding that the text creates.

The setting of this scene, both in time (autumn) and in place (the countryside), is used to provide a resonance which extends beyond the mere localised description. The metaphor of the nut thus fits appropriately into the poeticised context. This is also one of the few occasions in the book when Anne's role is perceived somewhat ironically. Although she is still the focus of sympathy, is she perhaps slightly self-dramatising in her retreat into poetry? More seriously we should note Anne's reaction to Wentworth's handing her into the carriage. *Persuasion* is a novel much concerned with the quality of sensation, and Anne responds violently to Wentworth's touch. The Crofts' conversation at the close of the chapter provides a further comment on the relationship between passion and constancy, and we need to be aware of how often Mrs Croft's speeches throughout the book make a positive contribution to the theme of love, as her role as model for Anne is slowly but surely established.

Chapter 11

Charles and Mary, Louisa and Henrietta and Anne go with Captain Wentworth on an overnight visit to Lyme Regis to see a friend of his, Captain Harville. Harville has a friend with him, Captain Benwick, who is in mourning for his late fiancée, Harville's sister, Fanny. That evening, in conversation with the grieving Benwick, Anne advises him as to the best way of coping with his loss.

Commentary
Persuasion works by creating a series of patterns, variations on the same theme. One of these is the repeated motif of loss, bereavement and misfortune. Benwick is one further example of a character who has lost a loved one. The pattern of which he is a part is complicated, and relates centrally to the theme of love and its need for financial security. Here we are invited to compare Benwick's demeanour with Harville's (who has shown great resilience in adapting to his injury and his new way of life) as well as with Anne's (who never shows how she suffers for the loss of Wentworth's love). Read the two descriptions of Benwick very carefully. The irony is most delicately handled so as to arouse our suspicions about the depth of his grief. Can you identify the phrases which create this effect?

Note the description of Lyme in this chapter. *Persuasion* is the only Austen novel that provides extended descriptions of landscape – why do you think it is included here? You should try to see how it fits in with the idea of change and the passage of time against which the human drama is played out. The wild, natural scenery is complemented by the more comfortable domestic interior of the Harvilles' home. Note as well how the rather serious tone of much of the chapter is lifted by the occasional tart comment from the narrator, as in the description of Louisa's decision to make the journey to Lyme, a decision that will prove to have unexpected consequences. Similarly, the author's remark about Mr Musgrove's concern for the condition of his horses clearly and comically sums up his priorities. Anne's 'amusement' at the end of the chapter is significant. This is the first time we witness her ability to laugh at herself. Lyme is going to prove a turning point in her story, and this reaction to events marks a change in the emotional absorption that has characterised her so far. Her function as the central character includes directing the reader to the ironies of certain situations.

Chapter 12

During an early morning walk with Henrietta, Anne passes a gentleman who clearly admires her. Seeing him again at the inn where they are both staying, she discovers that he is her cousin, the Mr William Walter Elliot who is heir to Kellynch Hall. Later, as the party takes a farewell walk through Lyme, Louisa falls down the steps of the Cobb and suffers severe concussion. She is left to recuperate at the home of the Harvilles with Mary as her nurse, while the others return to Uppercross to break the news to Mr and Mrs Musgrove. Wentworth then returns immediately to Lyme.

Commentary

This chapter marks a turning point in the relationship between Anne and Wentworth, although it is not realised by either of them. Coming exactly halfway through the book, it signifies a change of direction both in terms of action and tone. Even the comedy is more lighthearted than earlier in the novel: look at Henrietta's opening monologue, a delightful piece of self-exposure which lacks the savage bite of the initial satire of characters such as Sir Walter. Similarly, Mary's behaviour throughout is presented in an increasingly farcical style, reaching the heights of absurdity in the scene on the Cobb. From the very start, too, Anne emerges as a more positive figure than before when her beauty and vitality are appreciated by Mr Elliot and consequently noticed by Wentworth.

Louisa's fall from the Cobb is a crucial factor in this process of revision of Anne's qualities. In the ensuing panic of the accident, Anne is the only one who can retain self-control and can give practical advice. It is interesting to note that the men, traditionally figures of action and decision, are seen here as helpless, relying on Anne to take the lead. The irony of the episode partly springs from the fact that the character who is apparently the weakest and most passive emerges as being the strongest and most active. The contrast between Anne and Wentworth is especially marked. It is as if their conventional roles have been reversed here. Can you see how by the end of the chapter Wentworth's attitude towards Anne has altered in all sorts of subtle ways? The fall also serves a metaphoric function, for it is from this moment that Louisa falls in Wentworth's esteem, the accident being a direct result of her insistence on jumping down the dangerous steps. This contributes to the issue of firmness of mind and persuadability which is seen to be an increasingly complex matter as the book proceeds. Look carefully at Jane Austen's management of the scene on the Cobb. Although she is describing a potential disaster, the episode is highly comic. How do you think this is achieved, and why? Note the number of melodramatic or exaggerated terms that are employed, and the narrative stance of the whole, with phrases such as 'two dead young ladies' that undercut the gravity of the scene.

Chapter 13

Anne persuades the Musgroves to go to Lyme to be near Louisa, while she goes for her pre-arranged visit to Lady Russell. She accompanies Lady Russell to Kellynch Hall to call on the Crofts, where they discuss Louisa's accident and comment on the minor changes the Crofts have made in the domestic arrangements of Kellynch Hall.

Commentary
Once again we can see how the idea of 'persuasion' can operate – and be useful. Anne's encouragement to the Musgroves to go to Lyme is reassuring in their state of uncertainty. Anne's removal to Kellynch village gives us yet another perspective on egoism, for as she moves around the area she finds that different interests are uppermost in people's minds. Admiral Croft's comment that 'one man's ways are as good as another's, but we all like our own best', is a good key to this chapter, which shows the importance of tolerance and demonstrates that the significance of experience is relative and relies on the particular involvement of those most deeply concerned. Note how what is unspoken can be as important (or more so) than what is uttered aloud, as in the thoughts of Anne and Lady Russell on the subject of Wentworth and Kellynch and their individual ways of thinking about past events. This chapter brings out for the first time the contrast between Anne and Lady Russell in their response to the Crofts. Anne welcomes the refreshing nature of Admiral Croft's bluff and honest manner, a manner which Lady Russell would prefer to see tempered with more elegance and restraint. This minor incident serves to encapsulate the wider gulf in their attitudes to life. Similarly, the reference to the mirrors at Kellynch also serves to

define the difference between the outward-looking Admiral Croft and the inward-looking Sir Walter. Jane Austen's technique exploits each detail to the full.

Chapter 14

Charles and Mary return from Lyme and tell Anne how much she is admired by Captain Benwick. When Mr and Mrs Musgrove return they bring the Harvilles' children with them. Anne and Lady Russell call on the Musgroves and hear of Louisa's gradual recovery. Shortly afterwards, with very different feelings, they set out on their pre-arranged journey to Bath.

Commentary

This is another chapter apparently devoted to trivialities and non-events, but if we consider the thematic arrangement of the novel as a sort of jig-saw, we can see how the pieces of information conveyed here fit together and help to complete the overall design. We must bear in mind that the information about Benwick is imparted by Mary and Charles, who give differing versions of events: we need to work out the truth of the matter for ourselves and this can only be done in retrospect. The interchange between Mary and Charles is another example of the theatrical style of the comedy in the novel: their distinctive speech characteristics are balanced against one another in an effective and highly humorous contrast. The description of the visit to the Musgroves and the journey to Bath reinforces the idea of division of interests – between the Musgroves and Lady Russell, and between Lady Russell and Anne. Note how the remarks on Lady Russell's attitude to Bath reveal her as self-deceiving. Gradually, Anne's allegiances are taking positive shape.

Chapter 15

Anne finds her father and Elizabeth engrossed in the concerns of Bath and delighted to have renewed the acquaintance of Mr Elliot, who is also staying there. Later that evening, Mr Elliot calls and charms Anne with his good sense, judgement and manners.

Commentary

Once again the change of scene introduces us to a fresh perspective. The atmosphere of Bath infiltrated the closing paragraphs of the previous chapter. The sense of urban decadence is reinforced in this chapter: note how the language undergoes a subtle alteration to become more formal and indirect in the description of the Elliots' lifestyle, a gentle parody of their own stultification and reliance on convention. It is yet one more of the novel's ironies that the most alien locality should provide the setting for Anne's ultimate regeneration.

The comic description of Sir Walter and Elizabeth stresses their self-interest, intolerance and pettiness, and Anne's centralising perception ensures that we gain the correct moral perspective on the scene. Anne herself, however, does not escape the penalties of limited vision. Her opinion of Mr Elliot, for instance, is necessarily confined by her partial knowledge of him, knowledge which is not to be expanded until Chapter 21. The description of Mr Elliot is filtered through Anne's vision, and you should notice that it is her opinion, not the narrator's, that is offered. This is one of the few occasions in the novel when the two do not coincide. The book constantly gives us evidence which is prone to revision in the light of future events, and we are continually reminded of the inevitable blindness of individual human beings.

Chapter 16

Anne finds Mrs Clay's position assured in the Elliot household, and Mr Elliot also is a constant and welcome visitor. Sir Walter and Elizabeth eagerly renew acquaintance with some distant titled relatives, Lady Dalrymple and her daughter, Miss Carteret, who are newly arrived in Bath. Anne is contemptuous of this relationship, but Lady Russell and Mr Elliot both approve it for the status it confers on the family.

Commentary
This short chapter focuses on the disparity between artifice and nature in a variety of aspects, beginning with Sir Walter's reference to Anne's improved looks – he cannot believe that her beauty has a natural source! Anne's alienation from her family is re-emphasised, and her growth away from them and their set of values is particularly noticeable since her stay in the company of the Musgroves, Crofts, Harvilles and Wentworth, who seem direct and honest in comparison with the Elliots' reliance on the cachet of social class and wealth. The

satire here is directed towards exposing the chasm between the dead value system of the Elliot clan and the vital human element embodied by the others. Lady Dalrymple and Miss Carteret, mentioned so often, never appear directly, and they consequently seem empty, elusive figures, rather than real characters. The reiteration of their names shows the value Sir Walter attaches to title and status – he later discounts Mrs Smith because her name implies no heritage of consequence. We should note that Lady Russell, while despising the Dalrymples on personal grounds, still tolerates their acquaintance for the social rewards it brings. Where does this place her in the moral ranking order of the novel? Similarly, she approves of Mr Elliot because of his civility and elegance. Much of the description of him here is given from her point of view. As we learn subsequently, she is completely duped by his ability to act a part. It is a good exercise to re-read Mr Elliot's speeches in this chapter in the light of your knowledge of his duplicity. Can you see how carefully they are structured, and how they lack, for instance, the impulsive quality of Wentworth's language in Chapter 8? Try to analyse what it is that makes them seem unnatural.

Chapter 17

Anne discovers an old school friend, Mrs Smith, living in Bath, widowed, crippled and in straitened financial circumstances. The two quickly renew their old friendship, to the disgust of Sir Walter. Lady Russell tells Anne that she believes Mr Elliot is attracted to her, but Anne is suspicious of his uniformly polished charm and his lack of spontaneous energy and cannot return his affection.

Commentary

The division of this chapter into two separate sections encapsulates a moral division. Anne's relationship with Mrs Smith, based on a shared past and mutual interests, is balanced by the Elliots' shallow acquaintance with the meretricious Dalrymples. Note the stylistic difference between the two halves. The section dealing with Mrs Smith is straightforward and matter-of-fact in its manner of presentation; the second half of the chapter relies more on mockery to make moral points. Mrs Smith's frankness and her resilience in adverse circumstances are qualities greatly admired by Anne, and we are encouraged to draw a parallel between the two characters whose current situations are so different. It is important to recognise that Lady Russell's approval of Mrs Smith distinguishes her from Sir Walter's naked snobbery. Mrs Smith's presence here invites a further comparison, namely with Mrs Clay, for their situations as poor widows are not dissimilar; it also forces attention on Sir Walter's blindness to this. Although Mrs Clay is given no dialogue, her presence is oppressive throughout, and her name is cleverly suggestive of baseness.

The closing references to Mr Elliot's charms show Anne's refusal to succumb to Lady Russell's persuasiveness, despite the attractions of the argument she puts forward. This is one mark of the change she has undergone in the past eight years. Her silent dismissal of Mr Elliot's possible suit emphasises her percipience (especially with regard to his relationship to Mrs Clay) and her need for mutual honesty in friendship.

Chapter 18

Anne receives a letter from her sister, Mary, which informs her that Louisa Musgrove is engaged to be married to Captain Benwick, and also that the Crofts are in Bath. Anne is delighted, for different reasons, by both pieces of news. One morning, out walking, she meets Admiral Croft and discusses Louisa's engagement and Wentworth's reaction to it.

Commentary
Mary's letter is a brilliantly high-spirited comic exposure of character. Note how indiscriminate Mary is in her relation of events, and how her own self-interest, misplaced concern with social standing, and malice towards others dominate her perception. It is typical of Jane Austen's ironic method that one of the silliest characters is used as the bearer of such important information, and typical too that this information comes in the postscript to the main letter. The irony is intensified by the fact that Mary hopes to discompose Anne with the news about Benwick, whereas she has precisely the opposite effect. The focus throughout is firmly on Anne's thoughts and feelings about Wentworth, and Anne's internal reverie forms a stylistic and moral contrast with Mary's letter.

The Crofts now become vital characters. Not only do they represent the lifestyle that Anne finds so attractive and that is such a contrast with that of the Elliots and Lady Russell, but they provide access to Wentworth. We can see some evidence here of Jane Austen's original plan for the novel, when the Crofts were going to be the agents of Anne and Wentworth's ultimate reunion. However, their function in this respect remains symbolic, rather than actual. Once again note the references to Mrs Croft, her happiness in marriage and the equality of status she enjoys with her husband and his friends. The difficulties of spoken communication are highlighted by the closing conversation with Admiral Croft, when Anne is trying to find out what she can without asking directly. Jane Austen's ability to reproduce individual speech habits is shown to advantage here and with comic effect, as Admiral Croft's bluntness of language reflects his lack of discernment. He cannot imagine that Anne's carefully phrased questions and subtly directed remarks carry any meaning other than their surface value. The comedy is thus at Anne's expense as well as Admiral Croft's, and the chapter both begins and ends with an ironic illustration of the limitations of language.

Chapter 19
Captain Wentworth arrives in Bath and is visibly embarrassed to meet Anne and her family by chance one morning. From then on Anne's thoughts run on the likelihood of meeting him again.

Commentary
The comic focus of the opening encounter continues to exploit the barriers that language erects, as neither Anne, Mrs Clay nor Mr Elliot can be honest about their reasons concerning the ride in the Dalrymples' carriage. With hindsight, of course, we can deduce Mrs Clay's motives for wishing to walk with Mr Elliot, just as we can deduce what his are for choosing Anne – at this point he still thinks he has a chance of winning her. Nowhere in the book is the disparity between inward and outward activity more marked than in this short chapter, as Anne's violent feelings on meeting Wentworth are suppressed beneath the social codes of polite conversation. Her own inner turmoil is accurately rendered in the paragraph beginning 'She now felt a great inclination to go to the outer door'; its short phrases denote confusion, in marked contrast to the control of her uttered speeches. Given the placing of the narrative viewpoint in Anne's consciousness, we can only infer (again with hindsight) that Wentworth's feelings are equally powerful. With our knowledge of the

constraints of language we must assume that his restrained manner conceals an undercurrent of emotion. This is further developed through the snatch of reported conversation about Anne that Wentworth overhears. Note Jane Austen's absence of authorial comment regarding this incident. She is a most economical writer who includes nothing extraneous. In this instance the reader is expected to supply the missing information about Wentworth's response for full effect.

You should now be alert to the difference that has come over the presentation of Anne. By this stage in the novel she is frequently allowed to become a butt of mild mockery, as her desires are continually being comically frustrated. Because we have come to accept that the final outcome is inevitable, we can laugh at her misfortunes *en route* to the happy ending. In the scene with Lady Russell we see the ludicrous conjunction of Anne's romantic thoughts about Wentworth with Lady Russell's mundane concerns about the window curtains. The bathos is given added point through the mutual unspoken misunderstanding taking place – it all happens in Anne's imagination. This is not just a humorous incident, however; it also helps to underline the isolating effect of Anne's obsessive love for Wentworth.

Chapter 20

Anne meets Wentworth at a concert, and their conversation leads her to believe that he might still love her. They are interrupted by the social activities around them and especially by Mr Elliot, who makes constant demands on Anne's attention. Eventually Wentworth leaves the concert prematurely.

Commentary

This chapter forms a perfect example of Jane Austen's central method. It is apparently about nothing – a few trivial conversations at a social gathering – but on another level, that of Anne's emotional life, everything happens, as she sees for the first time the possibility of Wentworth's returning her love. As is characteristic of this novel, the serious matter is intertwined with comic episodes, as Anne and Wentworth's talk has to give precedence to the Elliots' self-importance and the fuss surrounding Lady Dalrymple. Jane Austen demonstrates the difficulties that beset romance in a social context. The phrase 'never had she sacrificed to politeness with a more suffering spirit' perfectly expresses the problem that is at the heart of the entire episode. Communication between Anne and Wentworth operates on two levels simultaneously: the language of polite conversation (about Louisa and about Lyme) and the more personal messages which are being transmitted beneath (about love, constancy and suffering). Note how the roles of Anne and Wentworth have become reversed. On this occasion, he is the one whose anxieties to be with her are transparent, and he is impeded by and jealous of her entanglement with Mr Elliot. In the past his intimacy with Louisa was the obstacle. We see as well how human relationships are determined by minutiae (look at Anne's contrivances to move her seat) and how sensitive the characters are to the slightest signs of encouragement or rebuff (why do you think Wentworth leaves so early?). In this delicate manoeuvring process, problems and confusions occur: Anne wants Wentworth to know that she loves him but cannot tell him so directly, and she can only surmise his feelings. When she asks herself, 'How was the truth to reach him?' at the end of the chapter, she sums up the difficulties of social and personal relations in this highly formalised society. These problems encountered by the characters are re-enacted by the reader. Jane Austen describes the outward features of the concert, and allows us to deduce the rest. Can you identify the signs by which she alerts us to the subtext here? Try to find all the words that relate to emotion, and in particular the dramatic presentation of Anne's consciousness.

Chapter 21

Anne visits Mrs Smith, who has heard rumours that Anne is to become engaged to Mr Elliot. When disabused, Mrs Smith tells Anne something of Mr Elliot's history and character, exposing him as mercenary and hard-hearted. She tells Anne that Mr Elliot used to be a close friend of her husband and that Mr Elliot was responsible for his ruin. Since her husband's death he has ignored Mrs Smith's appeals for help.

Commentary
The gossip with which the chapter begins emphasises the public nature of the stage on which Anne's personal drama is played out. Mrs Smith's reliance on rumour shows how truth becomes distorted and consolidates the view we have had earlier about signs and their

import: here Anne's most innocuous actions have been misinterpreted by others. Mrs Smith's lengthy story, which takes up the greater part of this section, is often seen by critics as being one of the weaker parts of the novel because significant events are relayed to us at second-hand rather than being directly enacted. The style of narration is also more conventional than we find in the rest of the text, lacking the distinctive Austen delicacy and ironic touch. It has an important thematic function, however, and does more than give us information about the past which will expose Mr Elliot as a villain. The revelations about his character have been carefully prepared for and contribute to the theme of the tenuous relation between appearance and reality. Anne is shocked to find how she has been deceived by Mr Elliot's plausible manner. Note the use of the letter here – it is the only time in the novel when we hear Mr Elliot's authentic voice.

Mrs Smith's own history fits in to the novel's thematic strand of youth, enthusiasm and unforeseen circumstances, and the connection between past and present time. The accidents that befell her in the past could not have been anticipated, but they have led directly to her present unfortunate situation. As a woman she is particularly vulnerable, open to exploitation and financially helpless. In all these aspects she can be compared directly with Anne. We should note again Mrs Clay's presence in all this. A minor character who is given very little to say, she yet has a dynamic effect on others' actions.

Chapter 22

After Mrs Smith's disclosures, Anne finds herself in an uncomfortable position regarding Mr Elliot, but his proposed departure from Bath for two days offers her some relief. Charles and Mary make a surprise call on the Elliots, having arrived in Bath the previous day with Mrs Musgrove, Henrietta and Captain Harville. Anne goes with them to their hotel, the White Hart Inn, to see Mrs Musgrove and Henrietta, who are soon entertaining a host of friends, including Captain Wentworth who arrives with Harville. In the midst of the commotion, Anne sees to her surprise Mr Elliot and Mrs Clay together in the street. Some minutes later, Sir Walter and Elizabeth come in and invite the Musgrove family, Harville and Wentworth to a party at their lodgings the following evening.

Commentary

The deceptions and self-deceptions of the Elliot household are the starting-point here, portraying the claustrophobic and insincere environment from which Anne will soon escape. We should note the neat structuring of the chapter which returns to this starting point. The resulting satire of the Elliots' and Mrs Clay's hypocrisy is quite merciless. Charles and Mary thus become transitional characters, uniting the qualities of the Musgrove and Elliot families, offering an active reminder of the events of the recent past, and preparing the way for the re-entrance of Uppercross concerns. Note Anne's speech to Charles about the parental approach of Mr and Mrs Musgrove towards their children's marriages. It is a bitter reminder of the attitude of her own father to marriage. The division of characters in the novel into two separate categories is strongly felt in this episode, when the energy and vitality generated by the Musgroves at the White Hart form a striking contrast to the stultifying, formal atmosphere of the Elliots' rooms. Similarly, their welcoming reception of Anne can be compared with the lukewarm greeting she received from her father when she first arrived in Bath. The text establishes a constant series of comparisons and contrasts, and we have to be aware of the novel's events as a continuum, and be prepared to see how each action relates to past occurrences. The narrative pattern, in its perpetual reference to the past, thus re-enacts one of the book's major concerns.

Wentworth's entrance reminds us of Anne's dominant interest, and the remarks about Mr Elliot recall the obstacles in the way of any direct declaration between them. Anne has now changed from the retiring, negative figure she cut at the beginning of the novel, and she can make skilful use of conversational opportunities to get her message across: thus her comment about not caring for an evening party. We should note, too, how she has clearly become a valued member of the Musgrove circle, no longer neglected and isolated as she was at the beginning of the book. She is still capable of misreading signs, however, and fails to understand the true significance of the meeting between Mr Elliot and Mrs Clay. Note Wentworth's comment about the past: this is the first time he has made explicit reference to his memories of eight years before. The importance of the past is ironically strengthened by Elizabeth's denial of it: 'The past was nothing' is a phrase that reveals her lack of understanding. The Elliots' invitation to Wentworth pinpoints his

dilemma, as he is torn between his contempt for the Elliots' condescension and his wish to be with Anne, and the gulf between the
two modes of living and their associated sets of values is emphatically
confirmed. The depth of Mrs Clay's guile, as seen in her defence to
Anne, cannot be fully disclosed until the final chapter. We as readers
are identified with Anne's perception, and it is only later that we
realise how the hints of Mrs Clay's treachery have been present
throughout.

Chapter 23

The following day, Anne goes to the White Hart where she finds a
large party assembled. Mrs Musgrove and Mrs Croft are chatting
about Henrietta's engagement, and Anne gets into conversation with
Captain Harville, while Wentworth, seated nearby, is writing a letter.
As Harville and Wentworth leave, Wentworth surreptitiously gives
Anne a letter in which he declares his love for her and asks her to
marry him. Anne is so visibly disturbed that the others think she is ill
and send her home. On the way she meets Wentworth. As they walk
together, they come to a full understanding at last. That evening at
her father's party, Anne tries to explain to Wentworth the reasons for
her decision to break with him eight years before.

Commentary
This is the longest and fullest chapter in *Persuasion*, and in it the main
ideas of the novel are fully articulated and brought to completion. It
begins with Anne in a state of agitation, and this heightened
emotional condition determines the significance of what follows.
Note particularly the sentence, 'She was deep in the happiness of
such misery, or the misery of such happiness'. The narrow margin
between ecstasy and suffering in Anne's intensity of feeling is
reflected in the subtle modulation of tones in the novel, mingling
comic and serious elements to suggest their mutual contribution to
the complex fabric of human experience.

The conversation Anne overhears between Mrs Musgrove and Mrs
Croft seems to relate directly to her own situation as they speak in
favour of young lovers marrying in the face of difficulties, and
condemn the uncertainties of long engagements. Despite their differences in intelligence and breeding, shown by their different speech
mannerisms, the opinions of the two women are closely aligned, and

they strengthen and support Anne's current views. Like Anne, we need to be sensitive to Wentworth's silent presence in all this, and how the slightest movement gives away his attentiveness. Why do you think Jane Austen refers to the pause in his writing at this point in the chapter?

Anne's own talk to Harville about constancy in love causes her to speak passionately about women's lives and their emotional dimension. She distinguishes between the nature of men's and women's experience, and the ways in which social constraints determine women's roles and deny them opportunities for distractions from personal matters. She also suggests that women's views have never been fully represented in literature and that men are consequently unaware of how deeply women can love. Although the conversation is stimulated by reference to Benwick, and Anne is speaking in general terms, she describes precisely her own situation, and it is this that encourages Wentworth to write his letter to her. Ironically, Anne, who has been so passive, has actively initiated the proposal of marriage she longs for. It is typical of Jane Austen's technique that at the emotional climax of the book she introduces a comic episode, here in the shape of Mrs Musgrove with her muddled, uncomprehending sympathy. This is the only scene in the novel when Anne's composure breaks down, and once more it is an ironic coincidence that restores her to Wentworth, as Charles unwillingly accompanies her home.

Read Anne's conversation with Wentworth most carefully. It produces sharply the effect of an enclosed private world which can exist in the most public surroundings. Unusually for a Jane Austen novel, it is the hero who has had to learn and grow in understanding, not the heroine, and Wentworth acknowledges his faults to Anne and describes the stages in his development – note how these are associated with the different localities in the book. In asserting the constancy of love he is prepared to admit to his own pride, and this is significant, given the variations on the theme of pride with which the novel deals. It is unusual, too, for Jane Austen to present such an intimate dialogue as this. Both here and at the end of the chapter the remarks about the wisdom of persuasion and a reassessment of the past are crucial. These passages need to be compared with the analysis of Anne's situation in Chapter 4. Why do you think Anne maintains that her early decision was right, given that it was so obviously wrong? In this question and its answer lies the key to much of the novel's meaning. You should note her emphasis on uncertainty and unpredictability, that 'advice is good or bad only as the event decides', and consequently her understanding that it is easy to be wise in retrospect. She also mentions duty and the presence of a moral conscience, and this relates to the motif of bonds between parents and children which is a recurrent feature of the text. The novel presents us with a reworking of a traditional literary conflict between love and duty, and depicts convincingly the impossibility of making a correct decision.

Chapter 24

Anne and Wentworth marry with the approval of their families and friends, including Lady Russell. Mrs Clay leaves Sir Walter's household for Mr Elliot's. Wentworth manages to have Mrs Smith's business affairs put to rights.

Commentary
In describing the response of Anne's family to her marriage, the final chapter returns to the overriding comic tone of the beginning of the book and reverts to some of those critical features. The question with which the chapter opens is particularly ironic, given the debate on this very issue we have just witnessed. Another irony is that Wentworth's personal fortune greatly exceeds Sir Walter's, and the baronet's condescension to his new son-in-law is therefore somewhat misplaced. Note the text's neatness of structure – we are back with Sir Walter and the baronetage, the point at which the story started. Throughout this final chapter, the narrative voice remains detached, in contrast to the intensity of analysis we witnessed in the previous episode. The loose ends of the story are tied up in an almost dismissive fashion, largely concentrating on the attitudes of the other characters towards Anne and Wentworth's engagement. Look at the change of tense in the description of Mrs Clay and Mr Elliot. Why do you think Jane Austen suddenly employs the present tense here when she has kept strictly to the past in the rest of the book? Although a comic point is being made about the general discomfiture of the Elliot clan and their vulnerability to opportunists, the change of tense humorously reflects one of the underlying themes of the book – the inability to see into the future. The narrator, who up to this point has been omniscient, is disclaiming responsibility for her characters, and

this helps to place the whole in a self-aware fictional framework. This use of the present tense is resumed in the closing paragraph, when total resolution is withheld. The tentative note in the last few lines of the book hints at possible future sources of anxiety. The mixture of serious and comic elements that has characterised this novel throughout thus persists to the last.

3 THEMES AND ISSUES

3.1 LOVE

Persuasion is first and foremost a love story. More than any other of Jane Austen's novels, this book deals centrally with a single love relationship, and this focus of interest is retained whatever else is being described. It is the progress of the love affair between Anne Elliot and Captain Wentworth that provides the main impulse for the plot.

In many ways, the love story is an unconventional one, and we need to be aware how much it differs from the sort of romantic ideal which figured in popular novels of the period and with which Jane Austen was all too familiar. Firstly, the protagonists, Anne and Wentworth, are an unusual choice for a literary heroine and hero. At twenty-seven and thirty-plus respectively, they contradict the youthful stereotype that was thought obligatory at that time. Remember how much is made of Anne's age in particular. When the novel begins she is thought to be quite firmly on the shelf and to have lost any chances of marriage after rejecting firstly Wentworth and then Charles Musgrove in her youth. At twenty-seven she is considered an old maid, and the other characters do not even begin to consider her as a possible candidate for Wentworth's hand in the face of the claims of the much younger Musgrove girls.

Secondly, Anne Elliot is not at all melodramatic in her manifestation of love. She is shown throughout the novel as capable of a deep and intense feeling, but she is also quiet and self-effacing. No one else even guesses at the secret passion she nurtures within herself. Her

but does not show it she nurtures it herself

love, silent and consistent, never wavers and is, until the very end of the novel, quite undemonstrative. This contrasts both with the displays of feeling we find in the protestations of the Musgroves, and with the self-indulgent behaviour of Captain Benwick. It also forms a sharp contrast to the family context in which Anne finds herself. Sir Walter and Elizabeth, incapable of feeling, are portrayed as sterile and ultimately callous in their inability to perceive her suffering.

The novel differs, too, from Jane Austen's earlier books, and from many contemporary fictions, in that the heroine does not have to undergo any process of moral education. Mature in years, she is also mature in understanding, and it is rather the hero, Captain Wentworth, who needs to be educated in order to appreciate her full value. The extent of his success in this field is perhaps questionable, and there are those who would argue that Wentworth never gains the degree of insight that makes him truly Anne's equal – but this is an issue you can consider further for yourself. Certainly Wentworth needs to develop emotionally. His interest in Louisa and Henrietta Musgrove stems largely from his response to their flattery, and he is clearly in error in thinking his feeling towards them is love.

The narrative movement of the novel from 'prudence' to 'romance' is also a reversal of the norm. Instead of providing us with the usual pattern of a young girl who falls in love with no thoughts for the social implications of her actions (as could be found in the pages of Fanny Burney's *Camilla*, for instance) Jane Austen gives us precisely the opposite. At nineteen, Anne is shown as being only too aware of the fact that her proposed marriage is 'unsuitable', and her sense of the potential problems the future might hold is what causes her to break the engagement. She does not in any way resemble the more usual figure of the rebellious heroine who disregards the advice of her elders. Rather she is a character who has a highly developed sense of social responsibility and controls her own passion accordingly. Instead of teaching its readers the lesson that the young must acquire prudence and take note of society's demands, the novel implies the opposite. It asserts the values of personal feeling above all else and suggests that young love should be allowed to flourish, despite the hardships that might be encountered. Note the conversation between Mrs Croft and Mrs Musgrove on this matter in Chapter 23, and Anne's silent endorsement of their comments.

Through the presentation of Anne and Wentworth, Jane Austen examines the nature of passion and its operation in a social context.

She depicts a society which is self-absorbed and whose daily round consists of mundane and often superficial activities. The Elliots, the Musgroves and Lady Russell spend their time visiting, walking, having dinner-parties and gossiping about their neighbours, the sort of routine existence that appears to lack all direction. In locating the main perspective of the novel within Anne Elliot's consciousness, however, Jane Austen is able to show us what goes on beneath the surface of this life. The mechanical occupations that take up Anne's time take up little of her emotional energy. The dramatisation of her inner life forms a brilliant exposé of the meaningless routines that comprise the business of Kellynch and Uppercross society, as we see the disparity between her inward feelings and her outward demeanour. It is love and love only that gives real meaning to life, suggests Jane Austen, and the characters who have no capacity for loving (such as Sir Walter) are satirised mercilessly.

At the opening of the book, Anne appears to survive only on the edge of existence, and for much of the action she does not seem to be a fully involved participant. She is rejected by Sir Walter and Elizabeth, and is made use of by Mary and the Musgroves. Her situation can be summed up by the answer to Wentworth's question in Chapter 8 as to 'whether Miss Elliot never danced? The answer was, "Oh! no, never; she has quite given up dancing. She had rather play. She is never tired of playing".' To play the piano for others to dance encapsulates Anne's removal from the mainstream of vitality. It is characteristic, too, of her position that this is an overheard remark. Rarely does anyone address her directly or listen to what she has to say. Instead she eavesdrops on others' conversations and gets her news at second hand.

When Wentworth returns to Kellynch, Anne's world, which for the past eight years has seemed only half alive, becomes transformed as the minute details of day-to-day events take on an added significance from his presence. Towards the end of Chapter 9, when Anne is annoyed by the attentions of her young nephew Walter, Wentworth lifts the child away. The scene is described as follows:

> her sensations on the discovery made her perfectly speechless. She could not even thank him. She could only hang over little Charles, with most disordered feelings. His kindness in stepping forward to her relief – the manner – the silence in which it had passed – the little particulars of the circumstance – with the conviction soon

forced on her by the noise he was studiously making with the child, that he meant to avoid hearing her thanks, and rather sought to testify that her conversation was the last of his wants, produced such a confusion of varying but very painful agitation, as she could not recover from, till enabled by the entrance of Mary and the Miss Musgroves to make over her little patient to their cares, and leave the room. She could not stay.

What we need to notice here is the wealth of meaning that Anne extracts from the incident. Wentworth's action produces in her a powerful response that might seem an over-reaction, given the casual nature of the scene. But Anne is able to analyse the subtlest details of Wentworth's behaviour in order to establish the precise state of the relationship between them. Her emotional involvement with Wentworth makes her hypersensitive, and consequently this directs us to the presence of a world consisting of complex and delicate undercurrents that forms the true plane of experience for Anne. The emphasis throughout this paragraph is on Anne's confused emotions, and the form of the passage re-enacts that confusion with its use of dashes and the long penultimate sentence which attributes to Wentworth a range of unspoken motivation.

Throughout the progress of this love affair the smallest details acquire significance, and we should note particularly the attention paid to physical detail. Anne is fully aware of the physical proximity of Wentworth in the passage quoted above, as she is in the scene at the Musgroves' dinner party when he comes to sit near her, on the same sofa, separated from her only by Mrs Musgrove's bulk. When he helps Anne into the Crofts' carriage after the long walk, she is alive to the fact 'that he had placed her there, that his will and his hands had done it'. *Persuasion* more than any other of Jane Austen's novels pays great attention to the nature of the physical world, and Anne's passionate awareness of Wentworth manifests itself in physical terms. The change in Anne's appearance as she becomes more intimate with Wentworth is made a central feature of the book. For Anne love is essentially revivifying. There are numerous references to Anne's loss of 'bloom' after her eight years of loveless existence. Wentworth is reported as saying that he would not have known her again, so physically altered did he find her, and Anne's lack of strength means that she tires easily when out walking. It is as if Anne is on the verge of fading away altogether were it not for Wentworth's timely reappearance. As the story proceeds, however, Anne's beauty also reasserts itself, and the beauty is seen as having its source in the renewal of love and hope that is taking place within her. In a book which deals fundamentally with the relation between public and private planes of experience, such a connection is clearly of great importance. Anne's looks are contrasted with the artificial quality of Elizabeth's handsome style, and at the concert in Bath a direct correlation is made between Anne's appearance and her feeling when 'her happiness was from within. Her eyes were bright and her cheeks glowed, – but she knew nothing about it.' The movement from darkness to light (note the words 'bright' and 'glowed' here) reflects the movement from Anne's emotional bleakness to a full reassertion of the potential of love in the book.

The emphasis throughout is directed towards Anne's rather than Wentworth's experience – much of the time we have to infer what he is feeling from the hints the text provides. But there is another angle on this. In Anne's conversation with Captain Harville in Chapter 23, she stresses the restricted nature of women's lives as distinct from men's. This is, she says, 'perhaps, our fate rather than our merit. We cannot help ourselves. We live at home, quiet, confined, and our feelings prey upon us.' While men are perceived as having continual diversion in their lives through their professions or their business, or even their outdoor sports, women's domestic lifestyle forces their attentions inward. Anne stresses the significance of the emotional life for women, and although we cannot take Anne's voice to be Jane Austen's, there is a degree of identification with her viewpoint in the novel that encourages sympathy with her ideas.

It is important to realise that the development of *Persuasion* demonstrates the values of individual feeling triumphing over the values of the hidebound, status-conscious society. It is seen as being Anne's (and Wentworth's) good fortune that after eight years he has become rich and successful. If anything this at first makes him seem an inaccessible figure to Anne, rather than a man to be eagerly sought after. We feel contempt for Sir Walter or Mary, both of whom are ultimately prepared to accept Wentworth because of his wealth and position. True love, it is suggested, exists independently of material advantage. Elizabeth Elliot is satirised for her interest in Mr Elliot, an interest based on his social assets only, and the social climber Mrs Clay is seen as morally unscrupulous in her attempts to catch a baronet for a husband.

The positive strength of the love between Anne and Wentworth is thrown into sharp relief by the portrayal of other romantic relationships in the novel. The passing attraction between Wentworth and the Musgrove girls, 'a little fever of admiration' as it is termed, bears no comparison to the single-minded quality of Anne's devotion. Louisa and Henrietta are captivated by the glamour of Wentworth's position, his good looks and his dynamic personality, and he is correspondingly flattered by their attentions. But his inability to choose between them indicates the lack of solid foundation to the relationship, and in observing the progress of Wentworth's interest, Anne is confident of being able to distinguish between this and what she remembers of his behaviour towards her when they were engaged.

A more interesting perspective on this is offered by Captain Benwick, whose presence in the novel provides far more than a convenient escape route for Louisa. When we first meet Benwick, he is introduced as the inconsolable grieving lover, but there are hints in this initial description that the quality of his feeling is shallow and that he is somewhat self-indulgently taking on the position of sentimental hero that his bereavement has conferred upon him. His penchant for reading sad books and the self-conscious demeanour he adopts suggest the role-playing element in his nature. We are invited to compare his situation with that of Anne, and his inconstancy to Fanny Harville's memory is a direct spur to Anne's claim that it is women who love 'longest, when existence or when hope is gone' (Chapter 23). Benwick's engagement to Louisa indicates the indiscriminating nature of their love, and by contrast helps to isolate the depth of passion which binds Anne to Wentworth.

The novel thus provides a series of relationships which act as a foil to the uncompromising central romance. Charles and Mary Musgrove, for instance, represent the sort of empty union which results when couples marry without love. Remember that Charles takes Mary only as a substitute, after Anne has refused him. Similarly inadequate is the affair between Mr Elliot and Mrs Clay, a gross parody of true romance – he is lustful, she is mercenary – so that together they are well suited. Note that all these men, Wentworth, Benwick, Charles Musgrove and Mr Elliot, are suitors for Anne's affection at some stage in the story. Wentworth is the only one who ultimately is not prepared to settle for second best. The relationships which are deficient in feeling are, however, balanced to some extent by the example of Admiral and Mrs Croft, whose ideal companionate marriage, based on a strong unwavering affection, is clearly a model for Anne to emulate. Throughout the main action of the book they are seen as a couple whose lifestyle might have been Anne's had she accepted Wentworth originally.

3.2 MAKING DECISIONS

All Jane Austen's novels are concerned with the relationship of the self to society. The subject of love and marriage, which is explored in each of her six major works, constitutes an examination into the ultimate amalgamation of personal feelings and social institutions. In *Persuasion*, through the story of Anne's initial rejection of Wentworth, Jane Austen investigates what happens when personal desire comes into conflict with the demands of society, and the subsequent decisions that have to be made; in so doing, the comic novel takes on near-tragic undertones, more fully articulated here than in any of her earlier books. *Persuasion* is perhaps Jane Austen's most mature novel in this respect. The awareness of alternatives permeates its presentation of scene and character, and the irony which is so strongly associated with Austen's technique here becomes deeply interwoven in the thematic texture of the novel.

The novel's title, *Persuasion*, in highlighting an abstract issue directs us to the conceptual underpinning of the book. Once again, the focus is on Anne Elliot, whose decision to reject Wentworth eight years before the main story takes place exemplifies the moral complexities which beset choice. This decision and Anne's yielding to Lady Russell's persuasion frame the present action of the novel. The episode is referred to at length both at the beginning (Chapter 4) and at the end (Chapter 23) of the book, and consequently informs our understanding of the events that form the bulk of the novel. It is important that we realise the impact of this framework, for it is crucial to the exploration of the relationship of past to present time with which the novel is concerned.

When at the age of nineteen Anne Elliot allows herself to be persuaded by Lady Russell to break her engagement to Captain Wentworth, she does so against her natural instincts. In examining this episode Jane Austen offers a version of the conventional conflict between love and duty which figured prominently in texts of the period. It is presented as a conflict between emotion and reason, heart versus head, and in Lady Russell we have the voice of reason, the voice that predominated in much eighteenth-century literature. Jane Austen is also re-working one of the oldest comic plots in existence, the thwarting of young lovers by the hard-hearted parent figure, but this traditional stock motif is given us here in a realistic form that highlights its application to the problem of individual lives.

It is perhaps too easy for us as twentieth-century readers to dismiss Lady Russell as a snob, given that her arguments to Anne are based largely on social criteria. In wanting the best for Anne, she sees the material disadvantages of Wentworth's suit: his youth, his lack of money, prospects or a wealthy family who could help support him. She is also an acute reader of personality, and in Wentworth she recognises certain danger signs. *Persuasion* frequently stresses the relativism of perception: that issues are not fixed and immutable but vary according to the perception of the onlooker. Anne admires Wentworth's courage, his brilliance, his wit and his relaxed approach to life. But for Lady Russell,

> his sanguine temper and fearlessness of mind, operated very differently on her. She saw in it but an aggravation of the evil. It only added a dangerous character to himself. He was brilliant, he was headstrong. – Lady Russell had little taste for wit; and of any thing approaching imprudence a horror. (Chapter 4)

This is not a simple case of blind snobbery but a sense of the effect of worldly experience on judgement. Lady Russell is presented as an intelligent and sensible woman, sensitive to Anne's needs. In wanting to guide her, she is also aware of the precariousness of a woman's position in an insecure world, and hopes to save Anne from the miseries that she sees might lie ahead. By most of the standards of her society, the advice Lady Russell gives to Anne is the right advice. One of the major ironies of the novel is that in this case it is also the wrong advice.

Ultimately the decision is Anne's, and in deciding to accept the advice of her friend, who is 'in the place of a parent', given the inadequacy of her own father, she shows her recognition of the possibilities of failure and misfortune in the proposed marriage. These include her sense of being a burden to Wentworth at such an early stage in his career. Not only is her action completely selfless, but it also denotes a maturity of understanding and a strength of character that are misunderstood by Wentworth, who sees her as a weak, malleable tool of her entrenched aristocratic family. When Anne explains the reasons for her decision at the end of the book, she talks about the problematic moral aspects of her situation. 'It was perhaps', she says to Wentworth, 'one of those cases in which advice is good or bad only as the event decides'. Individuals are asked to make choices in circumstances when the consequences of their choice are unknown and uncertain. Jane Austen is famous as a stringent moralist, but here she points up situations where the terms 'right' and 'wrong' are inappropriate, for only future events can determine the correctness of decision. The sense of the anguish that surrounds individual choice is treated with great compassion in this novel, which illuminates the difficulties that so often surround decision-making.

An added dimension to this aspect of Anne's situation comes with the introduction of Mrs Smith at a fairly late stage in the novel. It is characteristic of Jane Austen's method that often the most socially inferior characters are used to most telling effect (Miss Bates, in *Emma*, is an outstanding example of this). Although their current situations are superficially so different, Mrs Smith is used to provide an ironic comparison with Anne. Both characters made choices in their youth, and for both, the decisions proved disastrous. Mrs Smith's present unhappy condition is a direct result of her marrying for love; she could not have foretold the unhappy consequences that were to follow her decision – her husband's extravagance, his death, their debts and her ensuing illness. Her physical paralysis and imprisonment in the dark, cheerless room is a metaphoric reflection of Anne's emotional condition before Wentworth's return; her reliance on the gossip of Nurse Rooke compares with Anne's eavesdropping, while her resilience in the face of adversity is paralleled by Anne's silent fortitude.

Firmness of mind, then, the quality that Wentworth insists on in a wife, is seen in an ambiguous light. The novel is structured around a series of events where characters have to make decisions, and the variety of situation that these encompass builds up a sense of the multifarious nature of experience and the problems surrounding any attempt to judge according to preconceived principles: each case must be treated on its unique merits. The novel opens, in fact, with an act of persuasion, as Sir Walter needs to be cajoled into leaving Kellynch Hall. From this trivial instance of intolerance and a failure to listen to others' arguments, we move to the more serious analysis of Anne's broken engagement. This intermingling of the simple with the complex is a hallmark of Jane Austen's technique in this book, where the idea of there being an easily available moral solution to every problem has to be abandoned. This is the most difficult part of the lesson that Wentworth has to learn, and it is brought home most forcibly in his relationship with Louisa Musgrove.

Wentworth is compelled to reassess his understanding of the concepts of 'fortitude', 'resolution', 'decision' and 'firmness', all terms he applies to Louisa in Chapter 10 when he compares her to the hazelnut which, 'blessed with original strength, has outlived all the storms of autumn'. Louisa's strength, however, is revealed as stubbornness in the scene at Lyme when she insists on being jumped down the steps of the Cobb, not once but twice. Not only is Louisa's obstinacy exposed, but Wentworth is brought face to face with his own weakness, having allowed himself to be persuaded to humour her against his better judgement. It is important to note the flexibility of Jane Austen's use of terminology in the text: alternative words are used to provide a varying moral perspective on conceptual issues. As with Anne and Lady Russell's very different interpretations of Wentworth's qualities above, so in this episode 'confidence' can become 'self-will', just as Sir Walter's insistence on his own infallibility was earlier equated with intransigence and prejudice. This conceptual reassessment becomes even clearer in the aftermath of Louisa's fall, when all the characters who have up to this point seemed decisive and controlled now panic, and Anne, who has seemed the most passive, is the only one who can act rationally and can take the necessary practical decisions.

This episode also makes explicit the idea that there is an element of luck in determining the outcome of any decision. Louisa's fall from the Cobb is at first thought to be fatal, and it is only chance that saves her. The thematic irony thus continually presents us with alternative possibilities of events, and the part played in the novel by fortuitous circumstance is central to our understanding of its meaning. Louisa, for instance, could have died on the Cobb just as easily as she happened to survive. In contrast, had Mrs Smith's husband not died her fortunes would have been very different. It is chance that brings the Crofts (and Wentworth) to Kellynch; it is chance that helps Wentworth to win success at sea. It is chance that brings Benwick and Louisa together in Lyme, and chance that Mrs Smith happens to be in

Bath when Anne arrives there. Throughout the novel the idea that schemes do not go according to plan is ever present. This reinforces a pattern of actual or potential frustration, ranging from the most trivial (such as Mary's decision to accompany her sisters-in-law on their walk) to the more significant (such as the threat to Anne's ultimate happiness from the intervention of Louisa Musgrove).

Decision-making, then, is seen as a complex process, liable to be affected by all sorts of factors outside any individual's control. The novel presents us with a declining spiral of interpretations of 'firmness'. At one extreme we have Anne, who makes decisions based on a comprehensive understanding of the issues involved in each case, and whose behaviour throughout is characterised by her tolerance and her openness to others' points of view. The most unpleasant aspects of firmness are to be found at the other extreme in the self-will of Sir Walter and Elizabeth, who are incapable of accepting any attitudes or forms of behaviour outside their own narrow sphere. In Mr Elliot and Mrs Clay this firmness is manifested as self-interest, neither character being prepared to make concessions of any kind. It is reasonably easy to establish a moral attitude towards these extremes, but in realising that they form two sides of the same coin, we also need to be aware of the more problematic instance of a character such as Lady Russell. Her decisiveness does not have its source in malice, nor in self-interest. We are able to approve her motivation, although we regret its consequences, and it becomes a much more tricky matter to try and offer an absolute judgement on her behaviour.

Firmness is also directly related to the question of constancy in love, and in this realm of private feeling, Anne is single-minded. Again we have a range of examples to help illustrate the variety of experience encountered. Captain Benwick's attitude to falling in love, for instance, seems almost arbitrary: only shortly after his fiancée's death, he is attracted first to Anne and then to Louisa. Henrietta Musgrove, too, needs to be 'persuaded' of her love for Charles Hayter, once Captain Wentworth has arrived on the scene to distract her: she is a character for whom choice creates only anxiety. Mr Elliot, on the other hand, is prepared to woo Anne within six months of his wife's death, while simultaneously carrying on an affair with Mrs Clay. Strong-mindedness is thus presented at a range of levels and from a variety of perspectives. The understanding of its complex nature is a central part of Wentworth's educative process.

His forgiveness of Lady Russell shows his movement towards a position of maturity, recognising that moral absolutes are not always applicable in situations determined by subtle factors.

3.3 SOCIAL CHANGE

Persuasion begins with a savage attack on the insularity of the British aristocracy. The opening paragraph of the novel, in describing Sir Walter Elliot's fascination with the baronetage, depicts him as the representative of a society which is backward-looking and thus ultimately doomed to disappear. Sir Walter seeks comfort in books rather than from living human beings, and the obsession with history that he embodies reflects a self-absorption that is quite exclusive in its interests. It also reveals his refusal to adapt to the present or to the future, for Sir Walter can find solace only in the past, and that past, it is made quite clear, is dead and gone. Sir Walter has no sons to carry on his name, and his estate is entailed away from his daughters.

The subsequent description of Sir Walter and Elizabeth, which occupies the first three chapters of the book, provides the context for Anne Elliot's story. In satirising the family's snobbery, Jane Austen is doing far more than offering a humorous view of the distorted priorities of individual characters. The personal vanity and the family pride that Sir Walter, Elizabeth and later Mary exhibit, do of course contribute to the comic exposure of selfishness, extravagance and silliness which is Jane Austen's *forte*. The investigation of what constitutes true gentility is an abiding theme in all her novels, and the Elliots, although given the outward trappings of nobility (the inherited title, the stately home, etc.), are, with the exception of Anne, lacking in the consideration for others, sensitivity and humanity that defines the real aristocrat – the one who belongs to the aristocracy of feeling – in Jane Austen's world. The portrayal of Lady Catherine de Bourgh in *Pride and Prejudice* is a similar example of the vulgarity that can go hand in hand with rank, while Lady Middleton in *Sense and Sensibility*, like Elizabeth Elliot, imagines that formal civility is an adequate substitute for true politeness. These two characters, however, do not embrace anything other than their own foolishness, and we can laugh at them as comic creations in their own right. In *Persuasion*, on the other hand, Sir Walter and the rest of his clan share a set of values to such an intense degree that they create the impression of a whole section of society whose reliance on status blinds them to anything else.

Snobbery, therefore, is treated in this text with a directness and a ferocity lacking in Jane Austen's earlier works, and this is partly because here it is shown to be positively harmful. The Elliots' neglect of Anne is destructive – we have already mentioned the descriptions of her as 'faded' at the start of the story – and in excluding her from their family activities, disregarding her wishes, leaving her behind when they move house, they are effectively erasing her identity. In rejecting her in preference for such worthless acquaintances as Mrs Clay and Lady Dalrymple, Sir Walter and Elizabeth reveal their perverted values. Their emphasis on rank at the expense of human qualities becomes life-denying, and establishes the initial setting for the narrative which will move ultimately from decay to a resumption of vitality. This sense of a defunct world is encapsulated by the comment on the past thirteen years of Elizabeth Elliot's life, which have consisted of 'the sameness and the elegance, the prosperity and the nothingness' (Chapter 1) of a pattern of experience that is essentially sterile. Note, incidentally, the use of abstract nouns here: they add to the sense of vacancy and intangibility that is being conveyed. The reference to Elizabeth's past is also important, for the Elliots are always seen within the context of history, entrenched in a set of outmoded perceptions and unable to accept change. They cannot alter their lifestyle when circumstances demand it, and they are contemptuous of modern methods of behaviour (such as advertising) and of men and women whose families do not have eminent historic connections (such as Admiral Croft). The mirrors which embellish the walls of Kellynch Hall are emblematic of Sir Walter's inability to see beyond himself and show his blindness to the changing society with which he is surrounded.

Change is inevitable, however, and although the Elliots refuse to accommodate themselves to the progressive society in which they live, other characters will. The concerns of the Elliots appear peripheral in contrast with those of their neighbours, the Musgroves. Unpretentious and often imperceptive, individual members of the Musgrove family are still liable to be made the butts of Jane Austen's satire, but as a family they do display a genuineness of affection, a warmth and a sincerity that is endorsed by the value system of the text. They are also shown as flexible and responsive to change: 'The Musgroves, like their houses, were in a state of alteration, perhaps of improvement' (Chapter 5), states the narrator, implying a tentative relationship between change and progress. In addition we should note Mrs Musgrove's refusal to dwell on the past (*vis-à-vis* poor Dick), and her enthusiastic sanction of the young lovers, with their hopes for the future. The Musgroves' home, the Great House of Uppercross, forms a striking contrast to Kellynch Hall. Instead of adhering rigidly to a traditional regime of household management where umbrellas are kept in one position because that has been the habit for generations, the Musgroves abandon formality, and tradition is mingled with innovation, dead history with new life, as the portraits of Musgrove ancestors hang in a room where children are playing happily. Uppercross Cottage, the home of Charles Musgrove, has also been improved, with the addition of a 'viranda, French windows and other prettinesses', so that its modern appearance vies with the traditional grandeur of the Great House in attractiveness.

Persuasion presents its readers with a divided world. In direct opposition to the stultified Elliots, Dalrymples and Carterets, are the energetic sailors of the novel, the Crofts, Harvilles and, of course, Captain Wentworth. In Section 1 of this Guide, I mentioned the interest that Jane Austen, because of her brothers, always had in naval matters, and in *Persuasion* the life of the sailor carries with it suggestions of excitement, adventure and danger. Admiral Croft, who has reached the pinnacle of his career, has done so by his own efforts. His status is not dependent on inherited wealth, but on his enterprise and determination and his willingness to face danger and accept responsibility. These qualities have made his fortune, and the novel makes clear that he is not unique in this. As Mr Shepherd says at the beginning of Chapter 3, 'the present juncture is much in our favour. This peace will be turning all our rich Naval Officers ashore. . . Many a noble fortune has been made in the war'. Admiral Croft is a professional and as such a member of the new English aristocracy. Having represented his country abroad, he has now come home to settle permanently, and his succession to Kellynch Hall and Sir Walter's departure from it is one reflection of the changing society that was making subtle differences in all walks of early nineteenth-century life.

One of the major distinctions between Admiral Croft and Sir Walter is that Admiral Croft has acquired his position through personal hard work. Sir Walter, on the other hand, is fundamentally inactive, assuming that his rank entitles him to automatic privileges.

Instead of accepting the *status quo*, Admiral Croft, through the nature of his career and the procedures of promotion, challenges it, and much of his behaviour in the novel and conversations in which he is engaged focus on the process of change: for example, his alteration of the domestic arrangements at Kellynch, his discussion about taking women on board ship, and, most importantly for this novel, his attitude towards his wife. In a book which lays such stress on the value of personal qualities, the portrait of the Crofts' marriage makes a pointed contribution to the subject of changing mores. We need to set this union, based on a love match, against a background of arranged and socially advantageous marriages such as those which Sir Walter (and Lady Russell) seeks for his daughters. Mr Elliot was selected as a suitable husband for Elizabeth, as was Charles Musgrove for Mary, their qualifications being social, not personal. This arrangement whereby parental choice was a guiding factor in matchmaking was by no means an unusual practice in Jane Austen's day, and we need to understand this in order to appreciate how far the Crofts diverge from the accepted pattern. Mrs Croft's close companionship with her husband and her being seen to take the controlling hand, as she does when driving the carriage, for instance, mark the changes that were taking place on the domestic front as well as in the wider social sphere, and her presence in the novel is a useful marker of a more flexible attitude towards personal relations.

The principles represented by the Crofts are seen on a more subdued scale in the Harvilles, who also provide an image of quiet domestic harmony that is a corollary to the naval emphasis on the values of individualism. Harville's lameness, incidentally, acts as a tangible reminder of the perils of the seafaring life. The central embodiment, however, of the energy and progressive outlook that the navy stands for in this novel is undoubtedly Captain Wentworth. The qualities of confidence, fearlessness and intelligence that Lady Russell so distrusts in him are precisely those that define the new order that Anne ultimately adopts. Wentworth's sexual magnetism is also a significant feature of his portrayal. He is the representative of the life force in the novel, the absolute opposite of the dead world view adhered to so rigidly by Sir Walter. A term ascribed to him in the first description we have is 'ardour', and this suggests not just his enthusiasm for life, but his sexual vigour as well. Wentworth has a personal dynamism that attracts youth. Both Henrietta and Louisa Musgrove find him irresistible despite the age difference between them. He is also the main agent of Anne's regeneration. Like Admiral Croft, Wentworth has no inherited wealth, nor does he have any claim to a landed estate. His personal fortune has been earned, and almost all the references to him reinforce the idea of a man of action. His spontaneity is set against the life of habit that the Elliots find secure, and his impulsiveness is contrasted with the calculated behaviour of the suave Mr Elliot and the crude Mrs Clay. Wentworth, together with the other sailors, exemplifies the injection of new life into a moribund society. The choice of him as hero (he is the only one of Jane Austen's heroes not to come from the class of the landed gentry) endorses the feeling of openness to experience and the seeking of new potential that many of the book's encounters illustrate. Collectively the sailors are an active demonstration of the social revolution affecting the changes in the distribution of wealth and the nature of the English middle class at this period.

If, in *Persuasion*, the characters do form units of shared values, as I have suggested, where then do we place Lady Russell? It is evident that she is a more caring and sensitive individual than Sir Walter, Elizabeth or Mr Elliot. Anne's loyalty to her does not waver, despite the events that prove her judgement mistaken. Yet Lady Russell is an exponent of the traditional eighteenth-century philosophy that is questioned by the emergent individualist attitudes of Wentworth and the rest. Her reliance on reason as an infallible guide to action is shown to be mistaken in the world of a novel that presents us with the supremacy of emotion and instinct. This is not, however, a moral judgement in the text, but an observation, and it reflects the impact of Romantic thought on Jane Austen's writing. Rather, Lady Russell is a character whose resistance to change is presented with understanding in a climate in which certain changes could carry with them the threat of dispossession (as in the case of Sir Walter). The ending of the novel shows her willing to acknowledge her past errors and to accept Wentworth on his merits. She is distinguished from the Elliotts in this acceptance of Anne's marriage in that her motives lack self-interest. Like Anne and Wentworth, she finally bows to the force of feeling, her love for Anne outweighing other considerations, and in this she follows the main thematic thrust of the text.

4 TECHNIQUES

4.1 PLOT AND STRUCTURE

One of the most notable features of the narrative of *Persuasion* is its retrospective structure. The present action of the novel is framed by past events, and the issue of the relationship between past and present is vital to a complete understanding of the text. The way in which the time dimension operates forces us to question this relationship, for not only does the opening paragraph of the book draw our attention to the insistent impact of past events on the present consciousness, but, once Anne Elliot's dismal situation has been depicted, the scene moves rapidly backwards eight years in time in an attempt to explain the causes of her present misery. This time shift is crucial, for the past in this novel never recedes, although the way in which it is interpreted by different characters varies. All Anne's conduct towards Wentworth is governed by her knowledge of their past relationship, and her memory is what gives the reader a perspective on her current behaviour. This has obvious thematic relevance, and indeed it is often very difficult to separate technique from subject matter in analysing Jane Austen's novels, for the two are closely bound together, so that the structural organisation of the text is used in order to make a positive thematic contribution. Here, one incident from the past has determined the nature of Anne Elliot's future in ways she could not have envisaged, and the sense of the disproportionate effects of that one decision taken so long ago dominates the novel.

Despite the feeling of injustice that surrounds our perception of Anne's situation, *Persuasion* is a comedy. By this I do not mean to suggest that everything that happens in the book is intended to be funny, but rather that the overarching structure and the narrative approach of the novel conform to certain conventions that we normally associate with comic modes of writing. The direction of the story moves towards a happy ending, with the aspirations of the main characters realised in the concluding pages: marriage is one of the most familiar conclusions to be found in comic literature. The way in which the story is related also maintains a certain consistency, so that nothing really unpleasant occurs to interfere with the overall comic tone. Certainly *Persuasion* contains its fill of ridiculous characters and farcical episodes, but these are intermingled with more sombre, and often quite poignant, scenes, and it is this particular mixture of the lighthearted and the profound that makes *Persuasion* a more complex and mature novel than some of Jane Austen's earlier works.

Comedies can, and usually do, explore very weighty and sophisticated matters – in Section 3 of the Guide we discussed how some of Jane Austen's most penetrating ideas are developed in *Persuasion* – but the exploration is conducted in such a way that it never becomes too intense, and the underlying seriousness is not allowed to disturb the total comic decorum. In Jane Austen's novels this effect is usually achieved through irony, so that, however involved we might become at certain moments of the story, a certain level of artistic distance is established to which we always return, and even a character like Anne Elliot, who is one of Jane Austen's most sympathetic creations, does not totally escape the ironic focus that defines the approach of the whole.

Several of the structural motifs found in *Persuasion* are drawn from traditional narratives and well-known comic plots. For instance, the situation of Anne Elliot recalls in some ways the fairy tale of Cinderella. We have a lovely and virtuous heroine, whose beauty is hidden until a transformation takes place about halfway through the story, following which she is sought after by the man of her dreams. Like Cinderella, Anne is alone in the world. Her mother is dead and she is left in the care of her father and her two (morally) ugly sisters who try to prevent her marriage. At the beginning of the story, too, she is made the drudge of her sisters' households, performing the tasks that neither Elizabeth nor Mary wish to take on. I do not want to force the parallels too much, but most readers of *Persuasion* would agree that the story has a magical quality to it in its dramatic and almost miraculous reversal of Anne Elliot's fortunes.

Another feature of *Persuasion* which has its source in older forms of comic literature is the central conflict between generations that forms the mainspring of the action. The idea of elderly parent figures trying to thwart the desires of young lovers was a familiar motif even in classical times, and formed a staple plot device in Greek dramas. Here, as in most traditional comedies, Anne and Wentworth, who, we should remember, are originally very young lovers, manage to triumph over the barriers erected by Sir Walter and Lady Russell, and ultimately achieve their hearts' desire. Their progress to eventual fulfilment is not smooth by any means, and the introduction of rival attractions, here in the shape of Louisa Musgrove and Mr Elliot, is anoher favourite comic motif.

Persuasion in fact consists of several separate stories interwoven and balanced in order to create a pattern. The central love affair of Anne and Wentworth is highlighted by the various subplots which involve the different groups of characters. The romantic entanglements of Louisa and Wentworth, Louisa and Benwick, Henrietta and Wentworth, Henrietta and Charles Hayter, Mr Elliot and Elizabeth, Mr Elliot and Anne, Mr Elliot and Mrs Clay, and Mrs Clay and Sir Walter, compose a seemingly endless list of possible combinations. Together they give the novel its shape by providing a range of comparisons with the main relationship which helps to isolate its unique quality. In some ways Jane Austen is also giving us an ironic variant on the popular formats of romantic fiction of her day. By giving the main attention to her older lovers, and letting the young ones (Louisa, Henrietta, Benwick and Charles) take second place, she reverses the conventional plot mechanism, which tended to focus on youthful romance.

This sort of thematic density is typical of Jane Austen's structural method. Each individual episode in the novel is made to work overtime in its contribution to the various strands of argument which permeate the text, so that a complex intellectual pattern is created. For instance, much of the book is concerned with the clash between judgement and feeling. From the start, where Sir Walter's refusal to leave Kellynch shows his personal feelings triumphing over his judgement, through the more profound evaluation of Anne's rejection of Wentworth, where her judgement triumphs over her feelings, episodes are balanced so that the ideas are explored to their full potential. The title of the novel itself draws attention to a conceptual issue, and there are numerous incidents which show characters resisting persuasion or being easily persuaded. One result of this is the moral relativism of the text. The difficulties of making absolute judgements, based on principle, are exposed when individual situations are shown to be dependent on so many variables.

The story is set in four main locations, Kellynch, Uppercross, Lyme Regis and Bath, and these are used to chart the stages of Anne's progress towards fulfilment. Each setting focuses around a different group of characters and takes on their distinctive features. We have noted elsewhere how the novel reveals the parochialism and self-absorption of individual interests, and the four settings make this explicit. As Anne moves from one place to another, she finds people established in their own separate worlds, caring little for the concerns so often dominant in the others. Kellynch is based around the Elliots, their narrowness and sterility reflecting the restrictions on Anne's way of life. The move to Uppercross coincides with Anne's reunion with Wentworth, and centres around the Musgrove family, who, appropriately, represent both ties with tradition and an acknowledgement of the future. Lyme is the turning point in Anne's fortunes. Its situation by the sea complements the concentration on naval interests: Wentworth, the Harvilles and Benwick are all assembled here, and it is here that Anne's real personality begins to flower. The final setting, Bath, is a city, and it is here that the three groups of characters converge. Anne and Wentworth arrive at their mutual understanding in a communal, not an isolated, setting, surrounded by that range of personnel with which the novel deals.

Throughout *Persuasion* the progression towards eventual resolution is shadowed by potentially tragic incidents. In the preceding section of the Guide, we considered the regenerative nature of the narrative, how Anne's story reflects a movement from death to life. This positive narrative direction is fundamental in demonstrating the way in which the actual structure of the novel reinforces its thematic texture. But while bearing in mind this central impetus towards fulfilment, we need to notice, too, how there are continual reminders of divergent paths that the action could take. Because of the handling of tone in the novel, we are fairly certain as we read that the story will have a happy ending. Our curiosity is kept alive by our involvement in the process by which this is brought about, a process which contains numerous obstacles. So in *Persuasion* it is not so much *what* will happen as *how* it will happen that sustains the reader's interest. By weaving possible alternative scenarios into the text, Jane Austen is constantly suggesting that the final outcome is by no means inevitable, and the plot is used to strengthen the pattern of complicated experience that contributes to the final effect of the novel's vision. Plot therefore can be equated with meaning, and an examination of the structural organisation of the book provides a vital added dimension to any interpretation of it.

It is made apparent in the novel that Anne's eventual happiness is a result of fortuitous circumstances. In the initial stages of the story it does not appear that there will be any change in her life. On the contrary, after the disclosures of Chapter 4, it seems that her story is over, not just beginning. It is only by chance that Admiral Croft becomes the tenant of Kellynch Hall, and that subsequently Wentworth re-enters Anne's life. Throughout, the implications are that Anne's lover might never have returned. Even when he does so, he is determined to avoid her, and again it is contingency that throws them together and makes Wentworth realise Anne's true qualities. Louisa Musgrove's fall from the Cobb at Lyme is the crucial accident that swings the balance in Anne's favour, but it is made clear that the accident itself is only the last in a train of chance events that might never have happened, and had they not done so, Anne's opportunities of fulfilment might not have been realised.

Captain Harville's presence at Lyme is the first fortuitous circumstance in this chain: he has retired from the Navy because he has been wounded, an event that adds incidental support to the idea of the hazards of experience. Benwick's presence is another contributory factor: he is only there because of the death of Fanny Harville, an event that no one could have predicted, and it is because of this that he can ultimately remove Louisa as an effective rival for Wentworth's love. Next, Wentworth's interest in Anne is excited by the admiration of Mr Elliot, again a result of a random meeting. Louisa's eventual fall occurs, partly because of her self-will, but also because of the weather, the high winds that determine the occasion being beyond the control of any of the characters. You should look carefully at the description of the accident. Louisa is first thought to be 'lifeless', and it is only by chance that she does not die. Although we as readers are never in any real doubt about her survival (the extravagance of Mary's hysteria helps to keep the whole episode comic), the arbitrary nature of her recovery is made evident.

The novel keeps its focus on comic action and on episodes that mark a return to life (such as Louisa's adventure), but the counterpart to this is the awareness of death or loss that is pervasive. All the characters, apart from the Crofts and Wentworth, have suffered the loss of a loved one: a husband or wife, parent or child, brother or sister, or (as in Benwick's case) a fiancée. *Persuasion* is a book full of bereaved people, and the effect of this is to remind us of the dark, tragic element in experience that is the other side of the comic coin. Notably, all the really unpleasant events are recounted to us in abbreviated form, or passed on at second hand. The deaths of Lady Elliot, Dick Musgrove, Lord Russell, Fanny Harville, Mr Clay, Mrs Elliot and Mr Smith occur off stage, in most cases long before the events of the novel take place. The details are not dwelt on. If they are related, the tone of the narrative is dismissive or ironic, as in the instance of the tale of 'poor Richard', when we hear 'that the Musgroves had had the ill fortune of a very troublesome, hopeless son; as the good fortune to lose him before he reached his twentieth year' (Chapter 6). Once again we should remark the stress on the arbitrary quality of 'fortune'.

Similarly, when Mrs Smith is telling Anne the story of her husband's ruin, the weight of emphasis is given to the villainy of Mr Elliot, rather than to the sufferings of the victim. And because of the method of narration, the story within a story, the impact is reduced. We are not moved by Mr Smith's miseries, because they do not occur within the framework of events covered by the present action of the novel. Even the most extended account of real suffering, Anne Elliot's own story of the loss of Wentworth, is placed in the past, and although it is seen to affect the present situation, the immediate experience of distress is at a remove.

I began this section by considering the significance of recollection in the book's structure, and it is perhaps in this area that the novel approaches its most potentially tragic material. The subject of the blindness of individual human beings is more usually found in tragedies than in comedies. Here, by placing the central and most moving illustration of this in the past, Jane Austen can keep the comic elements dominant.

4.2 CHARACTERISATION

'You may *perhaps* like the Heroine, as she is almost too good for me', wrote Jane Austen to her niece, Fanny Knight, in 1817, about her latest creation, *Anne Elliot*. Of all Jane Austen's novels, *Persuasion* brings us the closest to the experience of a model character, but unlike that 'insufferable prig', as a critic once termed Fanny Price, the heroine of *Mansfield Park*, Anne Elliot manages to transcend her virtues and in spite of them to come across to readers as a warm and likeable human being. How does Jane Austen manage this?

Despite being the very antithesis of a conventional nineteenth-century heroine in her age and situation, Anne is the focus of the novel, and as such she is its most fully realised character. In a way, this sounds odd, for even though *Persuasion* probably gives us more physical description than any other of Jane Austen's works, we would still find it difficult to visualise Anne. We know that she is pretty, with 'delicate features and mild dark eyes', and that when the story begins she is 'faded and thin'. We also know that she recovers her 'bloom' as her love for Wentworth revives, but all this is somewhat intangible in comparison with the physical accuracy with which other nineteenth-century writers delineate their characters' looks. Here, for example, is the opening of the description of Mr Creakle, a schoolmaster in Charles Dickens's *David Copperfield*:

> Mr Creakle's face was fiery, and his eyes were small and deep in his head; he had thick veins in his forehead, a little nose, and a large chin. He was bald on the top of his head; and had some thin wet-looking hair that was just turning grey, brushed across each temple, so that the two sides interlaced on his forehead.

We never find this sort of precision or facial detail in Jane Austen's writing, but her characters nonetheless come alive on the page as recognisable individuals. What is more, although they are set firmly in an early nineteenth-century background, they are not confined to their historical period, but conform to universal types of personalities that are as familiar to us today as they were to Jane Austen's contemporaries nearly two hundred years ago. Once again, we have to look to the subject matter of the novel to give us a clue to its technique.

In communicating the importance of personal feeling in *Persuasion*, Jane Austen presents her heroine largely through the medium of her inner consciousness. Anne Elliot is realised not through externals of appearance or idiosyncrasies of manner, but through the way in which much of the story seems to emanate from her perception of events. *Persuasion* thus concentrates on the quality of subjective experience, and it is the close identification with her emotions and her thought processes that make Anne a convincing character. She is often both the subject and the agent of the narrative, and we are encouraged to identify with her point of view because so frequently the ironic perspective that controls other characters is absent in Anne. For example, when she hears Wentworth's opinion of her faded beauty, we actively participate in her response:

> 'Altered beyond his knowledge!' Anne fully submitted, in silent, deep mortification. Doubtless it was so; and she could take no revenge, for he was not altered, or not for the worse. She had already acknowledged it to herself, and she could not think differently, let him think of her as he would. No; the years which had destroyed her youth and bloom had only given him a more glowing, manly, open look, in no respect lessening his personal advantages. She had seen the same Frederick Wentworth. (Chapter 7)

This is both a description of Wentworth's appearance and a revelation of Anne's state of mind. Because of the absence of a controlling authorial voice here, we identify with Anne's perceptions. We accept her reliability as narrator, and are prepared to take her view of Wentworth as definitive. At the same time the passage gives us an insight into Anne's feelings of humiliation. Although written in the third person, it follows Anne's mental processes. This representation of the workings of a character's interior consciousness is a technique that we usually associate with more modern writers, with their greater familiarity with psychological analysis, but it is fundamental to Jane Austen's technique in *Persuasion* and it is what gives Anne her conviction as a character. Although the passage reads partly like speech, or even an argument – note the placing and function of the word 'No', for example – we should note that Anne is in fact silent. Often in Jane Austen's novels, the characters who say the least are those who think the most, and the realisation of Anne's unuttered thoughts gives the impression of a constantly alert personality, despite her seemingly passive role in other respects. Through the dramatisation of Anne's inner reflection, we as readers have access to information that is denied the other characters in the novel, who can only see and consequently have to judge on externals of behaviour.

As the story progresses, Anne gains in confidence. She remains a most acute and infallible observer and in that sense a moral touchstone for the reader, but she becomes less retiring and more outgoing in manner. Whereas the opening scenes of the novel show her as unloved, inert and marginal to the community life around her, the later scenes show her taking a more positive role, self-possessed and able to control her destiny instead of meekly accepting it. It could, for instance, be argued that in her conversation with Harville, Anne is aware of Wentworth's listening presence and her speech about women's constancy is a deliberately provocative move, designed to encourage his proposal of marriage. Some of the scenes in Bath also allow us to laugh at the heroine, who up till this point has been spared the force of Jane Austen's irony. When, glancing through a window, Anne notices Wentworth walking down the street, 'she now felt a great inclination to go to the outer door; she wanted to see if it rained' (Chapter 19). We also see her at the concert, like a nervous adolescent, trying to manoeuvre her seat to one at the end of a row so that there will be space for Wentworth to sit next to her should he choose to do so. The transformation that Anne undergoes in the novel results in her renewed beauty, her increased composure and self-assurance, and a return to a youthful approach to life. This is commensurate with the stylistic treatment of her character, which, while never withdrawing sympathy, allows a more relaxed view of her to surface.

Captain Wentworth is the natural corollary to Anne. It is often said of Jane Austen that she had no talent for depicting men. Certainly, she never shows men in situations alone together, although in this novel she perhaps comes closest to describing masculine feelings, both in the portrait of the friendship between Wentworth and Harville, and in the scene when Harville speaks to Anne about love. The interesting thing about Wentworth is that we see him largely through Anne's eyes. As in the extract quoted above, he is perceived in terms of the response he excites. Whereas in the characterisation of Anne we are shown the emotional fluctuations and the anxieties that dominate her experience, with Wentworth we see only the superficial manifestations of emotion, and have to guess at what lies underneath. Mostly our knowledge of this is retrospective, revealed only in the long scene between Wentworth and Anne in Chapter 23, but occasionally we glimpse the external signs of emotional confusion, as in Wentworth's obvious embarrassment at meeting Anne in Bath. His blushing, his awkward manner and his lack of ease in conversation are all signals to his inner emotional condition, but the only time we are allowed to witness this directly is through the medium of his letter of proposal.

I have said that Anne is an unusual choice for a heroine in Jane Austen's fiction. Wentworth is similarly unusual. In many respects he has the qualities missing from Jane Austen's more lifeless male figures, such as Edward Ferrars in *Sense and Sensibility* or Edmund Bertram in *Mansfield Park*, and it has been suggested that the strength of Wentworth's portrayal was inspired by Jane Austen's own experience of love. Certainly, Wentworth has a great deal of personal charm; he is attractive to women; he is careless and reckless in his attitude to life. In keeping with the ethos of the novel, this hero does not come from the moneyed classes and his family has no aristocratic heritage or social status. His personal qualities alone equip him for the heroic role. He is a man of action, an adventurer who has won fame and fortune through his brave deeds in war. He is also a man of feeling and sensitivity. His whole attitude to Anne in the first half of the novel testifies to the fact that he has not forgotten his love for her, nor his suffering when their engagement was broken. His memories are as acute as hers. We should also remember his acts of kindness, his compassion, for example, when he hands Anne into the Crofts' carriage. His passionate nature is implicit throughout his portrayal, but because of the controlling narrative perspective, we are only allowed to glimpse at this, and much of our information comes second-hand, conveyed through Anne's memories of eight years before.

However, despite all his sterling qualities, Wentworth is presented as being less mature than Anne. He has to undergo an educative process through the events of the novel before he can appreciate her as she deserves. Normally in Jane Austen's books it is the heroine who has to learn and be rewarded with marriage. In *Persuasion* it is the hero, and we have the acknowledgement of his enlightenment in the penultimate chapter, when he tells Anne how at Lyme he first realised his own errors in understanding.

The villain of the book, *Mr William Walter Elliot*, has his antecedents in contemporary romances, and we find his prototype in most of Jane Austen's earlier novels. Personable and manipulative, he comes from the same stable as Willoughby in *Sense and Sensibility*, Wickham in *Pride and Prejudice*, Henry Crawford in *Mansfield Park* and Frank Churchill in *Emma*. Like them, he gets off lightly. There is no doubt about his moral deficiencies. He is calculating, callous, self-interested and mercenary, all qualities that are the absolute antithesis of Wentworth's nature. Mr Elliot is also intelligent, sensitive, well-educated, and charming. Anne finds him attractive and entertaining and even considers (fleetingly) the idea of marrying him – note incidentally that the possibility of marriage to the villain is also present for the heroines in the other books I mentioned. Jane Austen takes the figure of the stock villain, but makes him into a more complex creation, as befits a novel where the difficulties of absolute categorisation are exposed.

The minor characters in *Persuasion* are treated quite differently from the leading romantic roles. *Sir Walter*, *Elizabeth* and *Mary* are comic portraits, presented with varying degrees of satiric intensity. The description of Sir Walter in the first chapter makes explicit Jane Austen's method with these highly ridiculous and consequently less realistic figures. 'Vanity was the beginning and the end of Sir Walter Elliot's character; vanity of person and of situation', states the author bluntly. The formality of the sentence structure echoes the artificiality of the character. Note too how the description begins with the emphasis on the abstract quality. Once this has been established, the rest of Sir Walter's behaviour develops and illustrates the central idea of 'vanity'. That one characteristic dominates and gives definition to his personality. Elizabeth is a less extravagant version of her father, but still reprehensible, her own humanity having been eroded by the overriding sense of family pride with which she has been imbued.

Mary is much more sharply drawn, but her conception is on similar lines. Taking her hypochondria as the starting point, the text develops her into a ludicrous figure of fun, less harshly because she is less dangerous than her sister Elizabeth due to the moderating presence of the Musgrove family, who refuse to tolerate her nonsensical attitudes. All three, however, are personifications of egotism in its various forms, and as such they are the butts of some of Jane Austen's most rigorous satire. They are the recipients of uncompromising moral criticism. The only other character who comes in for this sort of treatment is the insidious *Mrs Clay*, shadowy in comparison with the Elliot family, because we glimpse her only as a presence in the background, referred to by other characters but making little direct contribution to the dialogue herself.

Less extreme than the Elliots, but still within the comic range, are the characters of the *Musgroves*, the *Crofts* and *Captain Benwick*. Although we are given little direct description of them, they emerge as rounded human beings, not just as 'types', and they serve as examples of Jane Austen's skill in creating credible personalities with minimal information. We are given no insight into their minds. All are observed from the outside, and it is their behaviour and their use of language which gives them their distinctiveness. We know that Jane Austen had a great love of play-acting, and these characterisations demonstrate her use of dramatic resources. Mr and Mrs Musgrove are introduced somewhat plainly, as 'a very good sort of people; friendly and hospitable, not educated, and not at all elegant'. However, once Mrs Musgrove begins to speak – 'I make a rule of never interfering in any of my daughter-in-law's concerns, for I know it would not do: but I shall tell *you*, Miss Anne, because you may be able to set things to rights, that I have no very good opinion of Mrs Charles's nursery-maid' (Chapter 6) – she actively illustrates the qualities by which she has been defined, and by so doing she comes alive for the reader. Her speech lacks precision; she uses colloquial expressions; she relies on cliché; she is well-intentioned, but self-deluded. Both her limitations and her virtues are encapsulated by her language. Because her kindness and her genuine good-heartedness are beyond doubt, we can laugh at her sentimentality, her 'large fat sighings' over the death of her son, without any sense of moral condemnation.

We can see something similar at work with the depiction of Benwick, who is exposed as a poseur while still being given full recognition for his virtues. Incidentally, we should note that all these minor characters appear to us primarily from Anne's point of view. The information about Benwick is filtered through reports of him 'as an excellent young man and an officer', and his inconsolable state is first described by Wentworth. It is only when Anne sees Benwick that his real condition is made apparent. Unlike Mrs Musgrove, we never hear Benwick speak directly, but his style is conveyed via Anne's perception of it, and his mannerisms give him away: 'Captain Benwick listened attentively, and seemed grateful for the interest implied; and though with a shake of the head, and sighs which declared his faith in the efficacy of any books on grief like his, noted down the names of those she recommended, and promised to procure and read them' (Chapter 11). The emphasis on Benwick's gestures, which comply with the approved format of the conventional grieving lover, suggest the self-conscious nature of his pose, and this is supported by the use of the word 'seemed'. The concentration on his surface demeanour hints at the superficiality of his feeling, and his attitude is in deliberate contrast to Anne's, who in the same chapter has to force herself 'to struggle against a great tendency to lowness'.

Perhaps in some ways the most problematic character in the novel is *Lady Russell*. We have dealt with some of the problems regarding our response to her in Section 3 of this Guide. Lady Russell does not fit into any of the compartments we have discussed so far. She is the trigger of the main action of the novel, being the 'persuader' implied in the title, but she is by no means the villainess, although Wentworth thinks of her as such. This, of course, is one of the errors he has to revise. She is a well-meaning, sympathetic, but fallible human being, and although treated with great seriousness most of the time, is on occasions subject to the comic vision, such as the occasions when her thinking is clearly so divergent from Anne's, and comic misunderstandings arise.

In terms of its characterisation, *Persuasion* is a very unbalanced novel. Anne's central position both as subject and as narrative filter gives her a completeness that none of the other characters can match. Most of them serve a function as foils for her, their roles often working as ironic comparisons to expose their own inadequacies or to form a comment on Anne's personality. *Mrs Smith*, the often quoted weak link in the novel's scheme of characterisation, does seem sketchy in conception when contrasted with Anne, and appears to be present in the text in order to fulfil a particular thematic purpose. *Mrs Croft*, despite the fact that she occupies less space in the book than Mrs Smith, escapes this feeling of incompleteness. Mrs Croft operates as a model for Anne to aspire to. In the previous section we discusssed how the action of the novel continually holds out pointers to what might have been, had events turned out differently. Mrs Croft's presence does the same thing for character. Her lifestyle is one that Anne feels might have been hers had she become the wife of a sailor when she was young. Mrs Croft, because of her experience at sea, seems much older than Anne, but she is in fact only thirty-five, and in the same way that Anne feels when she visits the Harvilles that 'these would all have been my friends', Mrs Croft holds out a sense of promise for the heroine that counteracts the negative images produced by Mrs Smith or Mary Musgrove.

4.3 LANGUAGE AND STYLE

Virginia Woolf once said that of all great writers, Jane Austen was the most difficult to catch in the act of greatness. Because her novels deal with such ordinary situations and characters, readers often find it hard to define precisely how she transcends the commonplace ingredients she uses. Jane Austen chose her narrow canvas quite deliberately. The minutiae of everyday life provide the basic material with which she moulds her artistic vision. An extraordinarily disciplined writer, she makes each detail work purposefully, and invests the apparent trivia with meaning. In *Persuasion* this has a dual effect. Jane Austen both exposes the paucity of individual lives where characters are totally absorbed in superficial interests, while at the same time she shows how it is in the normal and the commonplace that true significance resides. This apparent ambiguity is endorsed by the stylistic duality of the novel. The language of *Persuasion* is both more ferocious in its satire and more romantic in its feeling than any of Jane Austen's other works. Its social comment is more sweeping than anything we find earlier, while at the same time it communicates a more personal view of experience.

The opening chapters introduce the satiric tone, and the first few pages establish a commanding authorial presence. When Jane Austen tells us that 'Lady Elliot had been an excellent woman, sensible and amiable; whose judgement and conduct, if they might be pardoned the youthful infatuation which made her Lady Elliot, never required indulgence afterwards', she creates a frame of moral reference against which behaviour can be judged. Look at the number of abstract terms in that quotation: 'excellent', 'sensible', 'amiable', 'judgment', 'conduct', 'infatuation', 'indulgence'; a conceptual structure is set up which determines the value system of the novel, and we should be aware how as readers our judgement has been conditioned and is ready for action by the time we get to the idea of 'infatuation'. Satire relies for its effect on a mutually understood moral framework in order to show deviations from an approved order, and this framework is defined right at the start of the book with the rational appeal to general attitudes. Although Jane Austen moves in and out of her characters' perceptions and often shows things from different points of view, she maintains this authorial stance as a basis to return to when necessary. Let us examine the opening sentence of Chapter 2 to see how this works:

> Mr Shepherd, a civil cautious lawyer, who, whatever might be his hold or his views on Sir Walter, would rather have the *disagreeable* prompted by anybody else, excused himself from offering the slightest hint, and only begged leave to recommend an implicit deference to the excellent judgement of Lady Russell, – from whose known good sense he fully expected to have just such resolute measures advised as he meant to see adopted.

The narrative voice alters here in the middle section of the sentence so that we are manoeuvred imperceptibly into Mr Shepherd's style of speech. This technique, whereby the voice of a character is represented while the author keeps the narrative in the third person, is known sometimes as 'free indirect discourse', and it is a technique that is fundamental to Jane Austen's ironic method in *Persuasion*. In this sentence we are alerted to it by the italics – there would be no need for these if Jane Austen were being straightforward – and by the sentence construction, which imitates Mr Shepherd's obsequious manner. This interplay of perspectives which we find throughout *Persuasion* exploits the disparity between varying levels of knowledge, and it is this that here exposes Mr Shepherd's self-interested manipulations.

A critic once used the phrase 'regulated hatred' in describing Jane Austen's style, and it seems particularly applicable to parts of *Persuasion*. The satiric elements are highly controlled and 'regulated', but they are often uncompromisingly direct. When we read that 'Mary was not so repulsive and unsisterly as Elizabeth' (Chapter 6), the word 'repulsive' seems exceptionally forceful in the context of the more oblique ironies found elsewhere, while the authorial comment on Richard Musgrove is savagely reductive:

The real circumstances of this pathetic piece of family history were, that the Musgroves had had the ill fortune of a very troublesome, hopeless son; and the good fortune to lose him before he reached his twentieth year; that he had been sent to sea, because he was stupid and unmanageable on shore; that he had been very little cared for at any time by his family, though quite as much as he deserved; seldom heard of, and scarcely at all regretted, when the intelligence of his death had worked its way to Uppercross, two years before.

Surprisingly perhaps for a book which takes romantic memory so seriously, Jane Austen here satirises sentimental nostalgia. The authority of tone is initiated with the word 'real' and then reinforced by the insistently formal organisation of the sentence, which makes no attempt to approximate the rhythms of natural speech. Note the careful arrangement of parallel phrases, balancing one another so as to build up the pattern of the whole. The detached narrative voice has an overview denied to any one particular character, and can thus afford to be quite ruthless in its demolition of Richard, of the Musgroves, of family affection, of mourning, and of the conventional treatment of death. It is this same voice which occasionally intrudes into the narrative with a general appeal to the reader. 'How quick come the reasons for approving what we like!' (Chapter 2), says the author before launching into an analysis of Lady Russell's motives. We are invited to share that privileged position of omniscience, removed from any involvement in the action in case we should be guilty of forgetting that this is only a fiction after all.

Often the satire works on a personal and more openly comic level, exploiting obvious differences in linguistic styles. Jane Austen is a most sensitive observer of language, and she exposes individuals who use it carelessly. It is appropriate that her heroine, Anne, is often silent, mistrusting unnecessary verbal utterance. Here is Elizabeth Elliot addressing Anne, who is about to visit Lady Russell in Bath:

'I have nothing to send but my love. . . You need not tell her so, but I thought her dress hideous the other night. I used to think her had some taste in dress, but I was ashamed of her at the concert. Something so formal and *arrangé* in her air! and she sits so upright! My best love, of course. (Chapter 22)

The comedy is produced by Elizabeth's thoughtless use of cliché. The empty message of affection she sends is revealed as meaningless by the discrepancy between her professions of 'love' and the malice of her real feelings. Her shallowness is intensified by her misplaced priorities – her petty comments on Lady Russell's clothes and on the way she sits – and by her own lack of self-awareness. The introduction of the foreign term 'arrangé' alerts us to Elizaabeth's own affectation – the precise quality she is condemning in Lady Russell. It is her language that gives her away, and Jane Austen is adept at varying style to fit individual character.

Anne's alertness to the dangers inherent in language is one of the features that distinguishes her from the others. When she listens to her father and Elizabeth describing the charms of Mr Elliot, she is sceptical because 'all that sounded extravagant or irrational in the progress of the reconciliation might have no origin but in the language of the relators' (Chapter 15). Language in Persuasion becomes a subject in its own right as forms of communication are explored. We should note, for instance, how much of the significant information communicated between characters in the book is conveyed indirectly, through rumours or second-hand reports (as when Mary tells Anne of Wentworth's remarks on her appearance), or accidental eavesdropping (such as Anne's overhearing from behind the hedgerow), or letters (Wentworth's proposal), rather than through direct confrontation.

All three of the above examples relate to Anne, and any consideration of the language and style of Persuasion needs to assess her position, for frequently the narrative voice is closely identified with hers. This identification is subtly achieved.The satire of the first three chapters destroys the credibility of the Elliots and Shepherds while at the same time gradually establishing Anne's reliability as observer, so that when in Chapter 4 we find Anne's perception dominant, we are content to accept it as trustworthy. The entry into Anne's inner consciousness is what gives the novel its 'romantic' atmosphere. The complicity with Anne's viewpoint creates a narrative position that gives credence to intuition and emotion as a basis for judgement. Anne's instincts are validated by the events of the novel, and the language dramatises her feelings. One example of how this is communicated within the controlled narrative structure is the description of Anne's condition after she has received Wentworth's letter:

The absolute necessity of seeming like herself produced then an immediate struggle; but after a while she could do no more. She began not to understand a word they said, and was obliged to plead indisposition and excuse herself. They could then see that she looked very ill – were shocked and concerned – and would not stir without her for the world. This was dreadful. Would they only have gone away, and left her in the quiet possession of that room, it would have been her cure; but to have them all standing or waiting around her was distracting, and, in desperation, she said she would go home. (Chapter 23)

Despite the fact that this is written in the third person it is Anne's response that determines the impressionistic effect of the whole. The break in the middle directs us to the Musgroves' misplaced concern – the colloquial 'for the world' places us momentarily in their speech idiom – but the fragmentary nature of the description indicates that this is a dramatisation of Anne's confused perceptions under stress rather than an indifferent, detached analysis. The brevity of 'This was dreadful' recreates the immediacy of Anne's emotion, with the word 'this', succeeded by ' *that* room', suggesting present involvement in the experience. It is a most personal description, following graphically the gradations of her reaction and highlighting her sensations.

The movement that we find in the novel between different points of view is used not just as an ironic vehicle but as a means of presenting the coexistence of different areas of consciousness. This interest in individual methods of perception is sustained throughout and contributes to the sense of the relativism of experience that we discussed in Section 3. It is not just Anne's feelings and mental activity that we capture, but on occasion those of several other characters as well. The beginning of Chapter 4, while maintaining the dominance of Anne's intelligence, recreates the thought processes of Lady Russell and Wentworth in such a way as to suggest the symmetrical nature of their influence on Anne's decision: they embody the conflicting forces of reason and passion, and the language is an important element in the methods of argument each adopts.

The duality of style which characterises *Persuasion* continues right up to the last page. It is typical of Jane Austen's technique that the final chapter returns to the detached omniscience of the opening, and we become distanced from characters with whom we have empathised previously. The penultimate chapter contains some intimate emotional exchanges between Anne and Wentworth, but the first sentence of the closing Chapter 24, 'Who can be in doubt of what followed?' at once inhibits our involvement with the characters by referring to general patterns of behaviour, and placing the protagonists on the same level as 'any two young people [who] take it into their heads to marry'. The author even intervenes to make an explicit comment on her creation – ' This may be bad morality to conclude with, but I believe it to be truth' – effectively reducing the characters to mere fictional figures who have lost their individual realities. The conclusion, however, does keep switching from the serious to the comic in its frame of reference. The irony of the novel is thus sustained in the continual awareness of alternative possibilities, and the happy ending is tentative in the vision of perfection it offers. In the mention of 'the dread of a future war' being 'all that could dim her sunshine', it is made clear that there is no such thing as an immaculate ideal. We are not allowed to forget the tragic potential of the comic conclusion in the explicitly qualified nature of Anne's happiness. The suggestions of the unseen and unknowable future are present throughout, and their inclusion here undermines the sense of completion that the rest of the chapter asserts. Irony is far more than a comic tool in this, Jane Austen's last novel: it becomes ingrained into the narrative method to such a degree that it acquires the status of a subject in its own right.

4.4 SETTING

I have already mentioned the ways in which the various locations of the novel contribute to its structural development, each indicating a separate stage on Anne Elliot's road to fulfilment. In most of Jane Austen's works the heroine takes a journey away from home (*Emma* is the only novel where this does not occur), a journey that reflects the heroine's progress from the protection of her family to a great self-reliance. Anne's travels in *Persuasion* also follow her emotional fortunes, as she rejects the Kellynch values in favour of the qualities embodied by Wentworth. *Persuasion*, however, is a novel that makes a more positive use of setting than Jane Austen's earlier works; the descriptions of surroundings are more detailed, and they help to develop a pattern of imagery that has great thematic resonance.

Scene-setting here is not confined to place alone. Autumn dominates the mood of the novel, and the numerous references to autumn create a metaphor for the current state of Anne's emotional life, which at the start of the story is apparently drawing to a chill wintry close, but which rediscovers the possibility of a new awakening. We should also note the time-scale of the novel's action: appropriately it takes us from winter to spring. Look at how Jane Austen uses the setting of time and place to add another dimension of meaning to the text. The walk to Winthrop, for instance, in Chapter 10, allows opportunity for comment on the human as well as the non-human aspects of the landscape. 'The tawny leaves and withered hedges' are ambivalent in nature, for the withered leaves also produce glossy nuts whose character, as Wentworth discovers, is deceptive. On the one hand, Anne meditates on 'the apt analogy of the declining year, with declining happiness, and the images of youth, hope and spring, all gone together', but on the other hand we have the active evidence of the harvest, 'where the ploughs at work, and the fresh-made path spoke the farmer counteracting the sweets of poetical despondence, and meaning to have spring again'. The imagery contains the duality that we have already noted as being a central constituent of the novel, and this pattern is echoed by the frequent references to Anne's beauty, faded at first, but ultimately returning to its youthful condition.

The novel's settings are also used to intensify our awareness of change. The picture we get of Uppercross village in Chapter 5 concentrates on the modernisations which have taken place, both in terms of the nature of the community and in the individual houses, internally as well as externally – note the remarks about Mary's drawing room, 'the once elegant furniture of which had been gradually growing shabby, under the influence of four summers and two children'. The arrangement of the sentence reiterates the balance of seasonal and human elements present elsewhere. The most marked example of this metaphoric use of setting is in the account of Lyme Regis, where the landscape overshadows the activities of the inhabitants and dwarfs human concerns. The description of Lyme's grandeurs has a pictorial quality that conforms to the contemporary Romantic taste in poetry and painting – as one critic has pointed out, Jane Austen uses the word 'romantic' quite without irony here – in its concentration on natural phenomena: the rocks, trees, tide and the cliff. The setting acquires a solidity, which testifies to the active presence of history and the inevitability of change as a part of the natural process of evolution.

Throughout the novel 'home' is seen as an arbitrary concept. Ideas about stability and change, land and sea, home and away, affect our perception of the importance of setting. The introduction of the sailors makes us realise that the concept of 'permanence' is not to be taken for granted, and that individual perspectives on experience are determined by travel or lack of it. The motif of travel relates closely to the idea of social change, indicating the existence of a world beyond the narrow confines of English country life. This extension of vision is important to the setting of the book's action, which is informed by a sense of unknown lifestyles and uncharted regions, and most significantly by the idea of discovery. We should note, too, the emphasis on outdoor activity for the sailors: they enjoy walking, riding and fresh air. This forms a sharp contrast with the atmosphere that surrounds the life of the Elliots, which seems to take place mostly in airless rooms, giving us a sense of restriction and confinement.

Critics have sometimes used the word 'poetic' to describe the style of *Persuasion*. This could refer to Jane Austen's reliance on certain repeated motifs and images to develop the pattern of ideas in the novel. The setting forms a part of this level of metaphoric suggestion, and it results in giving us a much sharper sense of the solidity of the physical world than we find in any other of Jane Austen's novels.

5 SPECIMEN PASSAGE

AND

COMMENTARY

5.1 SPECIMEN PASSAGE

The discussions of the preceding sections have isolated certain aspects of Jane Austen's approach to thematic and technical issues, but we have to recognise that this sort of critical division is an artificial exercise, intended only to guide you in your reading. Jane Austen herself does not separate the fictional elements in this way, but combines them to form a closely knit, coherent whole. The best way of observing this coherence is through close analysis of individual passages from the text. The extract I have chosen, as an example of how this sort of study can extend an understanding of the total work, comes from Chapter 8 of *Persuasion*. It shows us something of the range and the density of Jane Austen's art in this novel. She is a highly disciplined and extraordinarily economical author, and as readers we have to work hard in order to see how she exploits the resources of language to their full effect.

'I felt my luck, Admiral, I assure you,' replied Captain Wentworth, seriously. – 'I was as well satisfied with my appointment as you can desire. It was a great object with me, at that time, to be at sea, – a very great object. I wanted to be doing something.'   5
'To be sure you did. – What should a young fellow, like you, do ashore for half a year together? – If a man has not a wife, he soon wants to be afloat again.'
'But, Captain Wentworth,' cried Louisa, 'how vexed

you must have been before you came to the Asp, to see   10
what an old thing they had given you.'

'I knew pretty well what she was, before that day;' said
he, smiling. 'I had no more discoveries to make, than you
would have as to the fashion and strength of any old
pelisse, which you had seen lent about among half your   15
acquaintance, ever since you could remember, and which
at last, on some very wet day, is lent to yourself. – Ah! she
was a dear old Asp to me. She did all that I wanted. I knew
she would. – I knew that we should either go to the
bottom together, or that she would be the making of me;   20
and I never had two days of foul weather all the time I was
at sea in her; and after taking privateers enough to be very
entertaining, I had the good luck, in my passage home the
next autumn, to fall in with the very French frigate I
wanted. – I brought her into Plymouth; and here was   25
another instance of luck. We had not been six hours in the
Sound, when a gale came on, which lasted four days and
nights, and which would have done for the poor old Asp in
half the time; our touch with the Great Nation not having
much improved our condition. Four-and-twenty hours   30
later, and I should only have been a gallant Captain
Wentworth, in a small paragraph at one corner of the
newspapers; and being lost in only a sloop, nobody would
have thought about me.'

Anne's shudderings were to herself, alone: but the Miss   35
Musgroves could be as open as they were sincere, in their
exclamations of pity and horror.

'And so then, I suppose,' said Mrs Musgrove, in a low
voice, as if thinking aloud, 'so then he went away to the
Laconia, and there he met with our poor boy. – Charles,   40
my dear (beckoning him to her), 'do ask Captain Wentworth where it was he first met with your poor brother. I
always forget.'

'It was at Gibralter, mother, I know. Dick had been left
ill at Gibralter, with a recommendation from his former   45
captain to Captain Wentworth.'

'Oh! – but, Charles, tell Captain Wentworth, he need
not be afraid of mentioning poor Dick before me, for it
would be rather a pleasure to hear him talked of, by such a
good friend.'   50

Charles, being somewhat more mindful of the probabilities of the case, only nodded in reply, and walked away.

The girls were now hunting for the Laconia; and Captain Wentworth could not deny himself the pleasure of taking the precious volume into his own hands to save them the trouble, and once more read aloud the little statement of her name and rate, and present non-commissioned class, observing over it, that she too had been one of the best friends man ever had.

'Ah, those were pleasant days when I had the Laconia! How fast I made money in her! – A friend of mine, and I, had such a lovely cruise together off the Western Islands. – Poor Harville, sister! You know how much he wanted money – worse than myself. He had a wife. – Excellent fellow! I shall never forget his happiness. He felt it all, so much for her sake. – I wished for him again the next summer, when I had still the same luck in the Mediterranean.'

'And I am sure, Sir,' said Mrs Musgrove, 'it was a lucky day for *us*, when you were put captain into that ship. *We* shall never forget what you did.'

Her feelings made her speak low; and Captain Wentworth, hearing only in part, and probably not having Dick Musgrove at all near his thoughts, looked rather in suspense, and as if waiting for more.

'My brother,' whispered one of the girls; 'mamma is thinking of poor Richard.'

'Poor dear fellow!' continued Mrs Musgrove; 'he was grown so steady, and such an excellent correspondent, while he was under your care! Ah, it would have been a happy thing, if he had never left you. I assure you, Captain Wentworth, we are very sorry he ever left you.'

There was a momentary expression in Captain Wentworth's face at this speech, a certain glance of his bright eye, and curl of his handsome mouth, which convinced Anne, that instead of sharing in Mrs Musgrove's kind wishes, as to her son, he had probably been at some pains to get rid of him; but it was too transient an indulgence of self-amusement to be detected by any who understood him less than herself; in another moment he was perfectly

collected and serious, and almost instantly afterwards
coming up to the sofa, on which she and Mrs Musgrove
were sitting, took a place by the latter, and entered into
conversation with her, in a low voice, about her son, doing
it with so much sympathy and natural grace, as shewed the   95
kindest consideration for all that was real and unabsurd in
the parent's feelings.

They were actually on the same sofa, for Mrs Musgrove
had most readily made room for him; – they were divided
only by Mrs Musgrove. It was no insignificant barrier   100
indeed. Mrs Musgrove was of a comfortable substantial
size, infinitely more fitted by nature to express good cheer
and good humour, than tenderness and sentiment; and
while the agitations of Anne's slender form and pensive
face, may be considered as very completely screened,   105
Captain Wentworth should be allowed some credit for the
self-command with which he attended to her large fat
sighings over the destiny of a son, whom alive nobody had
cared for.

Personal size and mental sorrow have certainly no   110
necessary proportions. A large bulky figure has as good a
right to be in deep affliction, as the most graceful set of
limbs in the world. But, fair or not fair, there are unbe-
coming conjunctions, which reason will patronize in vain;
which taste cannot tolerate, which ridicule will seize.   115

5.2 COMMENTARY

This scene, at the Musgroves' house, depicts the first occasion that
Anne spends any time in Wentworth's company, and it is the first real
opportunity she has (and we as readers have) of observing him. It is
Wentworth's character, manner and behaviour that are the ostensible
focus of this episode, but as the beginning and the ending of the
chapter are located in Anne's consciousness, we should bear in mind
that our view of Wentworth is framed by our understanding of her
perception. This gives the scene its depth, and affects our reading of
Wentworth's first speech, which clearly demonstrates that the memory of his broken engagement is as keen for him as it is for Anne, in
his reference to 'that time'. The ironies of the passage come from the

skilful exploitation of differing levels of knowledge. As readers we have a privileged understanding, equal to Anne's, of past events, and can therefore interpret Wentworth's speeches in a way that the Musgroves and the Crofts cannot. Admiral Croft's reply, with its reductive generalities 'a young fellow like you' and 'if a man has not a wife', shows his limitations and indicates Wentworth's uniqueness: he does not fit into Admiral Croft's categories.

All Wentworth's speeches testify to this sharpness of memory. Look particularly at lines 64–6, where Wentworth refers to Harville's wife, and implicitly to his own state of singleness. The poignancy of these remarks (and incidentally the irony of Admiral Croft's initial reference to 'a wife') comes from what is unspoken: the short phrases indicate a world of feeling that is not articulated, and Anne's presence as hearer is what gives the speech its edge. Throughout the scene, Wentworth as speaker and Anne as listener are equally prominent participants, with a heightened sensitivity denied the other characters. This is never made explicit by authorial comment. The scene is essentially dramatic in conception – the characters are mostly realised through dialogue – and it is Anne's silent awareness that facilitates our comprehension. Line 35, 'Anne's shudderings were to herself alone', is one of the reminders of her exceptional position, and a pointer to the mute nature of the communication existing between herself and Wentworth to which the others are oblivious. It forms a marked contrast with Louisa's careless, somewhat childish outburst of lines 9–11, and it emphasises her isolation from the general conviviality around her. A central irony is thus established here between Anne's marginality in terms of social importance and her centrality as narrative filter.

Wentworth's long speech (lines 12–34) heightens these ironies. It shows his certainty about himself – look at the repetition of 'I knew' – and reiterates his acknowledgement of the influence of 'luck' on his career (a pervasive theme of his self-assessment, note lines 1 and 23), and the parallel stress on these creates a paradox of which he is unaware. The assertive character of the speech is rendered by the frequent use of 'I' and the range of active verbs, but Wentworth is not unpleasantly egoistic. He is modest about his own achievements – taking the privateers and the French frigate – and his extrovert performance here is qualified by his later kindness to Mrs Musgrove. His style of speaking is very intimate: he addresses other characters directly, invests his ships with identities and recalls specific names and places. Wentworth has the gift of being able to personalise experience – look at the aptness of his 'pelisse' comparison when talking to Louisa, and his spontaneous gesture of comfort towards Mrs Musgrove. It is typical of his optimism that he sees the storm as a piece of good fortune – many men would have interpreted it quite differently. But as well as being a revelation of his character, the speech relates crucially to the strand of the novel that deals with time and the relationship between past and present, a latent topic throughout this episode. Wentworth's confidence in his own abilities has been justified, but the remark in the closing lines about danger and death, although presented casually, alerts us to the possible alternative outcome of events. The added irony of 'nobody would have thought about me' is made more pointed by the subsequent immediate reference to Anne in the next line.

We are prevented from becoming too involved with the implicit pathos of the situation by the switch of attention in the next paragraph to Mrs Musgrove. At once the mood changes. Mrs Musgrove's sentimentality is made comic, partly because of the inconsistency of her attitude – despite all her professed interest in her son, she cannot remember the most fundamental details of his career – and her claim to Wentworth that 'we shall never forget what you did' (line 7) which has already been disproved. There is a tendency towards histrionics in her manner – her incessant use of the adjective 'poor' whenever she refers to Dick strips it of meaning – and this is highlighted by Charles's dismissive reaction. Mrs Musgrove's own resources of language are limited: she repeats phrases (lines 81–2), and her terminology and sentence structures are simple and childlike, reflecting a corresponding simplicity of personality. The comedy is intensified by her insistence on being heard, despite her family's attempts to ignore her, and by the discrepancy between her erroneous memories of Dick and the reality (lines 78–82). We should note, incidentally, how carefully patterned the whole passage is, as Mrs Musgrove's nostalgia is set side by side with Wentworth's and tacitly with Anne's.

Line 83 changes the perspective on the scene, and with this sentence we move more directly into Anne's vision of events. Starting with an objective view of Wentworth, the sentence shifts its emphasis towards Anne's response – the word 'probably' provides the link with Anne's thoughts, for an omniscient author would not be so tentative. Anne's percipience is remarkable: she notices details that less discerning observers miss, and the special nature of her relationship with Wentworth is kept to the forefront. Note how the angle of vision on people and events is continually adjusted. The comment on Mrs Musgrove in line 96, for instance, restores humanity to a character who was in danger of becoming a comic stereotype. This constant modulation of the narrative voice goes hand in hand with the modulations in tone and perspective that characterise the scene, and indeed *Persuasion* as a whole. We are not allowed to become complacent as readers but are forced to recognise the coexistence of multiplicity of simultaneous viewpoints.

It is certainly Anne's consciousness which has become dominant by the time we start the next paragraph. The word 'actually' and the hyphen of line 99 help to recreate Anne's mental agitation, and we see the significance of detail in determining the quality of individual experience. The second sentence, however, returns to a more detached overview. The abstract generalities, 'size', 'nature', 'cheer', 'good humour', 'tenderness', 'sentiment', 'agitations', place us in the hands of the all-knowing narrator, from whom we are prepared to accept the sort of concise, pithy reduction we get in the 'large fat sighings' of lines 107–3, and the directness of the dismissal of the 'son, whom alive nobody had cared for'. Note the effect of the change of tense in these last lines. By using the present tense, Jane Austen creates a basis for a shared contract between author and reader, and can then comment on the fictionality of her figures, such as Mrs Musgrove's absurdity, by relating this to a frame of reference of generally understood comic conventions. This is part of the modifying role of the author's voice in this novel, and it produces an uncertainty in the reader as to whether the events and characters are romantic or comic. The final sentence (lines 113–15) denies Mrs Musgrove her individuality yet again, and questions the balance between the reality of the world of the novel and its status as a fictional construct.

The variation of tones in the passage ranges from outward observation and satire (as in the depiction of Mrs Musgrove) to the dramatisation of personal feeling and the minutiae which affect it (as in the portrayal of Anne). In the continual movement from comedy to romanticism we are confronted with the mingling of these elements both in the style of the text and in the ambivalent view of events that results. The entire passage is heavily patterned, with the interwoven themes of love, fortune, uncertainty, and the complex relations between past and present time which permeate the novel as a whole.

6 CRITICAL RECEPTION

6.1 CONTEMPORARY VIEWS

Persuasion was published together with *Northanger Abbey* in a
four-volume set in December 1817, in an edition that included a
'Biographical Notice of the Author' by Jane Austen's brother,
Henry. The book took Jane Austen just twelve months to write, and
it was completed in the August before her death. We know that she
re-wrote the ending of the novel substantially. The original version
omitted the climactic proposal scene at the White Hart Inn, and
contained instead a scene at the Crofts' lodgings in Bath, where
through a series of blunders on Admiral Croft's part, Wentworth and
Anne are left alone together to declare their love. Clearly Jane
Austen was unhappy with this first version, which tended to emphasise the comic elements in the lovers' situation, and in writing the
concluding section in its final form, she created a fresh extra chapter,
which developed Anne's role, included her conversation with Harville about woman's constancy, and allowed greater scope for the
crucial analysis of the past. The novel now became a two-volume
work, with twelve chapters in each volume.

By the time *Persuasion* was published, Jane Austen had acquired
some reputation as a writer, partly as a result of the influential
author, Sir Walter Scott's assessment of her which appeared in 1815.
This was ostensibly a review of *Emma*, but Scott took the opportunity
to talk about Jane Austen's place in the evolving history of the novel.
In particular, he noted the realism which distinguished her work from
popular romances, and identified her as a significant 'modern'
novelist. Henry Austen's 'Biographical Notice' which accompanied

the publication of *Persuasion* did not attempt to emulate this sort of critical commentary, but it did testify to Jane Austen's genius, her powers of imagination, her literary education and her dramatic gifts. We have to realise that Jane Austen, although she always retained a select circle of admirers, was never a famous writer in her own time, and, according to Henry, never sought fame, but rather 'shrank from notoriety'.

Reviews of fiction in the early nineteenth century were not what we expect today. They included remarks on the author's life and often quoted chunks of the text in order to give potential readers a flavour of the work itself. There were only two real contemporary reviews of *Persuasion*, and of these, the one in the *British Critic* of March 1818 was rather grudging. The anonymous reviewer praised Jane Austen in general terms, but objected to *Persuasion* on the grounds of what he felt was its moral, 'which seems to be that young people should always marry according to their own inclinations and upon their own judgment'. In fact he dismissed the novel in a paragraph and instead gave his attention to the more accessible delights of *Northanger Abbey*. It has been suggested that he found it difficult to give unreserved approval to a novel which diverged so much from the accepted fictional norm. The review by Archbishop Whately which appeared in the *Quarterly Review* in 1821 was much more sympathetic to the innovations of *Persuasion's* style, and it remains one of the most important nineteenth-century assessments of the book. Whately realised that the moral elements in Jane Austen's work were not imposed didactically, but conformed rather to 'that unpretending kind of instruction which is furnished by real life'. For him, *Persuasion* was the finest of Jane Austen's books because it was the most mature in its vision, communicating a sense of the conflicting elements in experience in its mixture of tones and its serious approach to complex issues.

In spite of this, Jane Austen's work was never popular with the mass of nineteenth-century readers. It did not appeal to the prevailing Victorian taste for more dramatic, outspoken or socially wide-ranging novels than hers appeared to be. The novelist Charlotte Brontë exemplified the contemporary misunderstanding about Jane Austen: 'The Passions are perfectly unknown to her', she wrote disgustedly after the scholar and critic, George Henry Lewes, had advised her to read Austen's novels. 'Even to the Feelings she vouchsafes no more than an occasional graceful but distant recognition. . . Her business is not half so much with the human heart as with the human eyes, mouth, hands and feet'. Although *Persuasion*, together with Jane Austen's other books, was still in print throughout the century in Bentley's *Standard Novels* Series, it never found much favour with the general public. Like Charlotte Brontë, many readers saw in Jane Austen's writing only an outdated concern with trivial issues set in a world that had long disappeared, and failed to notice the breadth of her social criticism or her sensitivity to passionate undercurrents.

But, as a recent critic has pointed out, Jane Austen was always a critics' novelist, appealing to a refined and discriminating taste. An unsigned article of 1852 praised the range and quality of the characterisation of *Persuasion* which 'teems with brilliance'. W. H. Pollock wrote in *Fraser's Magasine* in 1860 that he thought Anne Elliot 'the most perfect in character and disposition of all Miss Austen's women'. And in a lengthy essay in which he compared Jane Austen with Shakespeare, George Lewes, the reputable critic, commented that *Persuasion* contained 'exquisite touches, and some characters no one else could have surpassed'. Yet *Persuasion* was always something of an anomaly for those who loved Austen's novels for their sparkling comedy. Even Lewes had to admit somewhat uncomfortably that, despite its merits, he thought *Persuasion* the 'weakest' of her books. In 1862, Julia Kavanagh in her *English Women of Letters* tried to explain the reason for the unusual sadness and tenderness of *Persuasion*. Her essay is the first real appreciation we have of Jane Austen's special insight into women's experience, and it leads directly into the more openly feminist readings of the novel which have gained credence in the later twentieth century. In Anne Elliot, Julia Kavanagh noted, 'we see the first genuine picture of that silent torture of an unloved woman, condemned to suffer because she is a woman and must not speak'. Julia Kavanagh also commented perceptively on the ambivalence of *Persuasion*'s ending, recognising that 'the sorrowful tone of the tale is not effaced by its happy close'.

In 1870, Jane Austen's nephew, James Edward Austen-Leigh, published a *Memoir* of his aunt in which he presented a portrait of her as a sort of gifted amateur, his 'dear Aunt Jane', who had a gentle sense of humour and could write some 'charming love-stories'. Almost immediately this view was contradicted in a substantial essay by the renowned Shakespearean scholar, Richard Simpson, whose critical approach to Jane Austen's writing was much more systematic and closer to our modern way of thinking than anything that had appeared earlier. Simpson saw Jane Austen's artistic career as one of continuous development, and *Persuasion* as a natural culmination of that development. He emphasised that her irony was a fundamental condition of her art, not just as a comic tool, as previous critics had asserted, but rather as a unique instrument of social criticism. Simpson related Jane Austen's moral position to the love interest in her novels, and he compared her genius in *Persuasion* to Shakespeare's in *Twelfth Night*, in its portrayal of an unspoken love and its distinctive combination of satiric and poetic elements. In this last novel, Simpson said, Jane Austen 'displays a poetical vein which her previous writings hardly justified one in suspecting'.

6.2 MODERN VIEWS

Most subsequent critics have, like Simpson, seen *Persuasion* as signalling a fresh departure in Jane Austen's method and way of thinking. In 1923, Virginia Woolf, herself an outstanding innovator in fictional technique, found *Persuasion* an elusive novel, characterised by 'a peculiar beauty and a peculiar dullness', which Woolf ascribed to Jane Austen's being 'a little bored' by the time she came to write it. Reading the work essentially from the point of view of one who was an author herself, Woolf noted the increased harshness of the satire in *Persuasion* and the greater sensibility of tone, and ascribed these changes to the fact that Jane Austen in this last novel 'is trying to do something which she has never yet attempted'. Woolf's approach is sensitive and personal, finding the source for the change in Jane Austen's own realisation of love, for the evidence of the book is that 'her attitude to life itself is altered'. For Virginia Woolf, Anne stands as Austen's mouthpiece in her experience of mute love.

With the publication in 1939 of Mary Lascelles' seminal work, *Jane Austen and her Art*, attitudes toward *Persuasion* began to focus more on the details of its technique and its place in Jane Austen's total career. Lascelles subjected Jane Austen's style and method to rigorous scrutiny and concluded that, far from being a naive and artless writer, Jane Austen was in fact a scrupulous, disciplined and conscious artist, whose approach to writing was informed by wide reading and scholarship. She put forward the view that it was meticulous self-criticism that made Jane Austen re-work the ending of *Persuasion*. By dealing with Austen's six novels as a complete *oeuvre*, Lascelles was able to identify recurrent patterns and motifs that the texts shared and could thus isolate with precision those features which distinguished *Persuasion* from the rest. This sort of attention to textual detail has dominated readings of the novel ever since, and it marks one of the main differences between nineteenth- and twentieth-century critical methods.

By the middle of the twentieth century, then, *Persuasion* was accepted as one of Jane Austen's most challenging works. Several critics concentrated on the presentation of its heroine as offering the key to its interpretation. Marvin Mudrick in *Jane Austen: Irony as Defense and Discovery* (1959) felt that the depth of Anne Elliot was 'the sustained depth of projected and implicit personal emotion', and that her centrality was what made the novel an essentially romantic rather than a comic work, for

> *Persuasion* is concerned, not focally with the operation of the social world upon men's characters, but with the emotional resistance that men put up against the perpetual encroachments of the social world. The whole pattern of the novel is one . . . of resistance and tension.

Similarly, C. S. Lewis, in an essay in *Essays in Criticism* in 1954, focused on the isolation of Anne Elliot and the consequent suffering she endures. These qualities were for him what defined *Persuasion*'s distinctiveness and gave it its romantic tendency, and this view of Anne as the embodiment of individualist values has had a powerful effect on shaping subsequent readings.

Several recent approaches to the novel have been historically or sociologically based. Alistair Duckworth (1971) was one of many who saw *Persuasion* as reflecting the social changes of the time, addressing itself 'to the predicament of the isolated self responding to social deprivation', and the Kellynch scenes as an indication of the break-down of an old structured society. Another critic, Marilyn Butler (1975), working along similar lines, has argued convincingly that Jane Austen was fully cognisant of the contemporary ideological debates of her day, and that *Persuasion* was a response to specific current issues. Captain Wentworth could thus be seen as 'a classic case-study of a modern-minded man from the conservative point of view', and the whole form of the novel reflected the tension of a society in conflict. Anne's story was essentially that of a nineteenth-century novel, but contained in an eighteenth-century satiric framework, and this fictional tension embodied the tension of the intellectual climate of Jane Austen's day.

The increasing body of feminist criticism has also offered provocative insights into the text. Some of this has focused on Jane Austen's position as a woman writer in a period when conditions of literary production were restricted, and have seen Anne's speech to Captain Harville about the male domination of literature as a cry from Jane Austen's own heart. Another line of argument has taken Anne Elliot as the embodiment of women's suffering, her passivity and silence emblematic of women's roles generally. Certain critics have felt that of all Jane Austen's novels, *Persuasion* dramatises most forcefully the distinctive nature of female experience and its divergence from masculine modes of life. Its emphasis on the inner life of the feelings and Anne's description of women's inevitable introspection is the basis for this view. An alternative school of thought has suggested that it is Anne's rationalism which gives her confidence. Her ability to act authoritatively at Lyme helps her to take control over her own destiny. The lesson she has to learn in those lonely eight years is one of action and initiative rather than passive self-sacrifice.

Whatever line of interpretation they adopt, critics now are generally agreed that *Persuasion* is one of the finest of Jane Austen's novels. It is more sombre in mood and more complex in its organisation and narrative patterns than earlier works, and this is evidence of a greater maturity on the part of the author. As Virginia Woolf said about Jane Austen, we cannot tell what new directions *Persuasion* marked, for 'the most perfect artist among women, the writer whose books are immortal, died "just as she was beginning to feel confidence in her own success".'

REVISION QUESTIONS

1. Consider the significance of the title in *Persuasion*.

2. How far would you you agree that 'there are . . . comic scenes and comic characters in *Persuasion* but its inner orbit and final effect are not comic'?

3. Comment on Jane Austen's use of the different locations in *Persuasion*.

4. In what sense can the episode at Lyme Regis be termed the climax of *Persuasion*?

5. Through a close study of specific extracts, comment on Jane Austen's satiric technique in *Persuasion*.

6. *Persuasion* has been called the most 'poetic' of Jane Austen's novels. What evidence do you find for this view?

7. Is Anne Elliot too perfect?

8. How and with what effect does Jane Austen handle the time dimension in *Persuasion*?

9. Not all the characters in *Persuasion* are paid the same degree of attention. Can you justify the inclusion of the following: Henrietta Musgrove, Elizabeth Elliot, Captain Harville, Mrs Croft, Mrs Smith?

10. 'She was satisfied with life and society, as she saw them around her', wrote Julia Kavanagh of Jane Austen in 1862. Does your reading of *Persuasion* support this view?

11. In 1928 a critic wrote of Jane Austen that she was a writer 'whose experience of life was so narrowly and so contentedly confined, whose interests were at once so acute and so small, whose ideals were so irredeemably humdrum'. How damaging to its final scope is the limited subject matter of *Persuasion*?

12. Do you think that the portraits of the male characters in *Persuasion* are unsatisfactory?

13. Consider Jane Austen's treatment of love and romance in *Persuasion*.

14. Comment on Jane Austen's management of the narrative perspective in *Persuasion*.

FURTHER READING

Christopher Gillie, *A Preface to Jane Austen* (London: Longman, 1974).

Mary Lascelles, *Jane Austen and her Art* (Oxford University Press, 1939).

Marghanita Laski, *Jane Austen and her World* (London: Thames and Hudson, 1969).

David Monaghan (ed.), *Jane Austen in a Social Context* (London: Macmillan, 1981).

Norman Page, *The Language of Jane Austen* (Oxford: Basil Blackwell, 1972).

LeRoy W. Smith, *Jane Austen and the Drama of Women* (London: Macmillan, 1983).

Brian Southam (ed.), *Persuasion and Northanger Abbey: Casebook Series* (London: Macmillan, 1976).

Tony Tanner, *Jane Austen* (London: Macmillan, 1986).

Mastering English Literature
Richard Gill

Mastering English Literature will help readers both to enjoy English Literature and to be successful in 'O' levels, 'A' levels and other public exams. It is an introduction to the study of poetry, novels and drama which helps the reader in four ways - by providing ways of approaching literature, by giving examples and practice exercises, by offering hints on how to write about literature, and by the author's own evident enthusiasm for the subject. With extracts from more than 200 texts, this is an enjoyable account of how to get the maximum satisfaction out of reading, whether it be for formal examinations or simply for pleasure.

Work Out English Literature ('A' level)
S.H. Burton

This book familiarises 'A' level English Literature candidates with every kind of test which they are likely to encounter. Suggested answers are worked out step by step and accompanied by full author's commentary. The book helps students to clarify their aims and establish techniques and standards so that they can make appropriate responses to similar questions when the examination pressures are on. It opens up fresh ways of looking at the full range of set texts, authors and critical judgements and motivates students to know more of these matters.